NEXT-DAY JOB INTERVIEW

prepare tonight and get the job tomorrow

MICHAEL FARR

jist
Works
America's Career Publisher

PART OF JIST'S HELP IN A HURRY™ SERIES

NEXT-DAY JOB INTERVIEW

© 2005 by JIST Publishing, Inc.

Published by JIST Works, an imprint of JIST Publishing, Inc.
8902 Otis Avenue
Indianapolis, IN 46216-1033
Phone: 1-800-648-JIST   Fax: 1-800-JIST-FAX   E-mail: info@jist.com

Visit our Web site at **www.jist.com** for information on JIST, free job search tips, book chapters, and ordering instructions for our many products! For free information on 14,000 job titles, visit **www.careeroink.com**.

See the back of this book for additional JIST titles and ordering information. Quantity discounts are available for JIST books. Please call our Sales Department at 1-800-648-5478 for a free catalog and more information.

Acquisitions and Development Editor: Lori Cates Hand
Project Editor: Heather Stith
Interior Designer and Page Layout: Aleata Howard
Cover Designer: Katy Bodenmiller
Proofreader: Jeanne Clark
Indexer: Kelly Henthorne

Printed in the United States of America
10 09 08 07 06 05   9 8 7 6 5 4 3

Library of Congress Cataloging-in-Publication Data

Farr, J. Michael
    Next-day job interview : prepare tonight and get the job tomorrow / Michael Farr.
        p. cm. -- (JIST's help in a hurry series)
    Includes bibliographical references and index.
    ISBN 1-59357-131-3 (alk. paper)
    1. Employment interviewing. 2. Job hunting. I. JIST Works, Inc. II. Title. III. Series.
    HF5549.5.I6F368 2005
    650.14'4--dc22

                                                    2004030334

ISBN 1-59357-131-3

This Short Book Can Make a Big Difference

This small book has a specific purpose: to help you quickly improve your job interview skills. Despite all the advances in hiring technology, most people still get hired—or, more often, screened out—based on a personal interview. Of course, you need the necessary job-related skills to be considered for a job, but how well you do in the interview often makes the difference in whether you get a job offer or not. But can you easily improve your interviewing skills? And if you can, will it help you get a better job than you might otherwise? The answer is "Yes!" And this book shows you how.

You can learn techniques to present yourself more effectively in an interview. Most people can dramatically improve their interviewing skills in a short time. My experience with thousands of job seekers is that just a few hours of learning and practice is often enough to make a big difference.

You will learn more than just how to interview. Although this book emphasizes interview skills, it also covers how to get interviews in the first place, follow up after an interview, and negotiate your salary.

You can find a good fit without being phony. Unlike some interviewing experts, I believe that you should tell the truth in an interview. I don't believe it is either necessary or good to manipulate a prospective employer into hiring you based on phony interviewing skills. I encourage you to identify the skills you have and then clearly define where and how you want to use them. If you present those skills to the right people, you will get the right job for the right reasons.

The interviewing techniques are based on research and common sense. Although I certainly have my opinions, many of the methods I suggest have a solid basis in research and have been field tested over many years by me or by others. My interest has always been to find more effective ways to help people get good jobs in less time. Often, research just seems to back up what makes sense.

I wish you well in your interviews and your life.

Contents

A Brief Introduction to Using This Book

Ideally, the best way to prepare for an interview is to research the organization and the job for a week or two, get a good handle on your qualifications and experience, and carefully consider your responses to the tough questions that might come up. But you have an interview tomorrow and have been too busy to prepare before now. How can you get up to speed tonight?

1. **Read some quick tips that will dramatically improve your performance.** The tips in chapter 1 will quickly help you improve your interviewing skills—enough for an interview later today or tomorrow. They provide a short but thorough interviewing course and will teach you far more than most of your competition knows about interviewing.

2. **Know thyself.** Use the worksheets in chapter 2 to quantify what you can do so that you can present yourself well to the interviewer.

3. **Get the inside scoop.** Chapter 3 shows you some quick ways to find information about the job and the organization that will come in handy in the interview.

4. **Know how to answer the key interview questions.** Chapter 4 shows you a process for answering most interview questions, and then uses it to create solid answers to 10 frequently asked problem questions.

5. **Be ready to handle unusual questions in a positive way.** Chapter 5 gives advice on handling difficult questions about your personal situation and convincing an employer why you should be hired over someone else.

6. **Go out and get more interviews.** You have to *get* interviews before you can do well in them. So, as soon as you learn to improve your interviewing skills, your next task is to get lots of interviews. Chapter 6 provides a quick review of the most effective methods I know to get more and better interviews.

7. **Follow up.** Often the key to turning interviews into offers is following up effectively. Chapter 7 shows you how to keep yourself foremost in the interviewer's mind.

8. **Negotiate your salary.** The interview went well, and you've been offered the job! But how can you be sure you're getting the salary you're worth? Chapter 8 gives you insights on how to handle this stressful phase of the interview process.

There is no need to read these materials sequentially; just spend time where you think the biggest payoff is for you and where you need the most help. So what are you waiting for? Jump right in and start improving your interview skills right now!

Chapter 1

Quick and Essential Tips for Tomorrow's Interview

The interview is the most important 60 minutes in the job search. A great deal is at stake, yet the research indicates that most people are not well-prepared for the interview process. This lack of preparation can be good news for you, because reading this book can help you substantially improve your interviewing skills, thereby giving you an advantage over the majority of job seekers.

I have observed many employers who are willing to hire people who present themselves well in an interview over others with superior credentials. This chapter is based on substantial research into how employers decide on hiring one person over another. Although the interview itself is an incredibly complex interaction, I have found that there are simple things you can do that make a big difference in getting a job offer. This chapter presents some of the things I have learned over the years, and I hope you find them helpful.

Six Common Types of Interviews

Before we get into the specifics of how to succeed in interviews, it might help you to read about the different forms your interview might take. Your first interview is likely to fall into one of these six categories:

- **The preliminary screening interview.** In the most common type of first interview, you meet with a person whose role is to screen applicants and arrange follow-up interviews with the person who has the authority to hire. Other times, you may meet directly with the hiring authority, whose primary focus is to eliminate as many applicants as possible, leaving only one or two. These one-on-one interviews are the focus of the techniques presented in this chapter.

- **The group or panel interview.** Although still not as common as the one-on-one interview, group interviews are gaining popularity. You could be asked to interview with two or more people involved in the selection process, or I've even known of situations where a group of interviewers met with a group of applicants at the same time. Many of the techniques used in this book work well in these settings, too.

● **The stress interview.** Some interviewers intentionally try to get you upset. They want to see how you handle stress, whether you can accept criticism, or how you react to a tense situation. They hope to see how you are likely to act in a high-pressure job.

For example, this type of interviewer might try to upset you by not accepting something you say as true. "I find it difficult to believe," this person might say, "that you were responsible for as large a program as you claim here on your resume. Why don't you just tell me what you really did?" Another approach is to quickly fire questions at you, but not give you time to completely answer, or to interrupt you mid-sentence with other questions.

I hope you don't run into this sort of interviewer, but if you do, be yourself and have a few laughs. The odds are the interview could turn out fine if you don't take the bait and throw things around the room. If you do get a job offer following such an interview, you might want to ask yourself whether you would want to work for such a person or organization. (If you turn down the job, think of the fun you could have telling them what you think of their interviewing technique.)

● **The structured interview.** Employment laws related to hiring practices have increased the use of a structured interview, particularly in larger organizations. In this type of interview, the interviewer has a list of questions to ask all applicants and a form to fill out to record the responses and observations. Your experience and skills may be compared to specific job tasks or criteria. Even if the interview is highly structured, you will likely have an opportunity to present what you feel is essential information.

● **The reality interview.** Some organizations now use a method commonly called "reality interviewing." Instead of asking traditional questions like "What is the best way to handle customer complaints," the reality interview asks more specific questions like "Tell me about a situation when you handled a customer complaint. Be specific in telling me what you did and what happened as a result." The objective is to get applicants to present specific things they did in the past as a way to indicate how they are likely to handle similar situations in the future. You might be asked very specific questions like "Your sales efforts resulted in a large order to an important customer. The order needs to go out right away to meet the customer's needs, but the accounting department has put a freeze on this account due to slow payments in the past. What would you do and why?" These kinds of questions provide excellent opportunities for well-prepared job seekers to present the skills and abilities that are needed for the job they want.

- **The disorganized interview.** You will come across many inexperienced employers who will not do a good job of interviewing you. They may talk about themselves too much or neglect to ask you meaningful questions. Many employers are competent managers but poor interviewers, and few have had any formal interview training. The best way to handle these interviews is to present the employers with the skills you have to do this job. Give them the answers they need to hire you even if they neglect to ask the right questions.

Eight Important Actions for Interview Success

What do you want to accomplish in your next interview? Although most people know that the interview is important to both you and the employer, few job seekers have a clear sense of what they need to accomplish during those critical minutes. Later chapters describe interview techniques in more detail, but what follows will help you get a quick understanding of the most important things to do in an interview.

1. Make a Positive Impression

Employers rarely hire someone who makes a negative first or later impression. These tips can help you make a positive impression before and during your interview.

Before the Interview

What happens before the interview is extremely important, although it's often overlooked. Before you meet prospective employers, you often have indirect contact with those who know them. You might even contact the employer directly through e-mail, a phone call, or correspondence. Each of these contacts creates an impression.

There are three ways an interviewer may form an impression of you before meeting you face-to-face:

1. **The interviewer already knows you.** An employer may know you from previous contacts or from someone else's description of you. In this situation, your best approach is to acknowledge that relationship, but treat the interview in all other respects as a business meeting.

2. **You have contacted the interviewer through e-mail or by phone.** E-mail and the phone are important job search tools. How you handle these contacts creates an impression, even though the contacts are brief. For example, both contact via the phone and contact via e-mail give an impression of your language skills and ability to present yourself in a competent way; e-mail also quickly communicates your level of written communication skills. So if you set up an interview with the employer, you have already created an impression, most likely positive enough.

   You should call the day before the interview to verify the time of your meeting. Say something like: "Hi, I want to confirm that our interview for two o'clock tomorrow is still on." Get any directions you need. This kind of call is just another way of demonstrating your attention to detail and helps to communicate the importance you are placing on this interview.

3. **The interviewer has read your resume and other job search correspondence.** Prior to most interviews, you provide the employer with some sort of information or paperwork that creates an impression. Sending a note, letter, or e-mail beforehand often creates the impression that you are well-organized. Applications, resumes, and other correspondence sent or e-mailed in advance help the interviewer know more about you. If they are well done, they will help to create a positive impression. (For quick advice on putting together an effective resume, see *Same-Day Resume,* another book in the *Help in a Hurry* series.)

> **Tip:** *Administrative assistants, receptionists, and other staff you have contact with will mention their observations of you to the interviewer, so be professional and courteous in all encounters with staff.*

The Day of the Interview

To make a good impression on interview day, use these tips:

- **Get there on time.** Try to schedule several interviews within the same area of town and time frame to avoid wasted time in excessive travel. Get directions online (from www.mapquest.com or similar sources) or ask for directions from the receptionist to be sure you know how to get to the interview and how long traveling to the interview will take. Allow plenty of time for traffic or other problems and plan on arriving for the interview 5 to 10 minutes early.

- **Check your appearance.** Arrive early enough to slip into a restroom and correct any grooming problems your travel may have caused, such as wind-blown hair. You would be surprised how many people go into the interview with grooming problems such as messed-up hair or smudged lipstick on their teeth. Use a breath mint or gum just to be on the safe side. Do not spray on perfume, cologne, or hair spray right before the interview because many people are sensitive to chemicals and scents.

- **Use appropriate waiting-room behavior.** As you wait for the interview to begin, keep in mind that it's important to relax and to look relaxed. Occupy yourself with something businesslike. For example, you could review your notes on questions you might like to ask in the interview, key skills you want to present, or other interview details. Bring a work-related magazine to read or pick one up in the reception area. The waiting room may also have publications from the organization itself that you may not have seen yet. You could also use this time to update your daily schedule.

- **Be prepared if the interviewer is late.** Hope that it happens. If you arrive promptly but have to wait past the appointed time, that puts the interviewer in a "Gee, I'm sorry, I owe you one" frame of mind. If the interviewer is 15 minutes late, approach the office manager or administrative assistant and say something like: "I have an appointment to keep yet today. Do you think it will be much longer before (insert

> **Tip:** *Identify things you habitually do that may create a negative impression and avoid doing them during the interview. For example, don't slouch, crack your knuckles, mess with your hair, or spread your papers across the next seat. Do not smoke, even if the employer invites you to do so.*

interviewer's name) will be free?" Be nice, but don't act as though you can sit around all day, either. If you have to wait more than 25 minutes beyond the scheduled time, you may want to ask to reschedule the interview at a better time. Say it is no problem for you and you understand things do come up. Besides, you say, you want to be sure Mr. or Ms. So-and-So doesn't feel rushed when he or she sees you. Set up the new time, accept any apology with a smile, and be on your way. When you do come back for your interview, the odds are that the interviewer will apologize—and treat you very well indeed.

- **Be particular about your dress and appearance.** How you dress and groom can create a big negative or positive impression, especially during the first few seconds of an interview. With so many options in styles, colors, and other factors, determining the correct approach can get quite complex. To avoid the complexity, follow this simple rule: Dress and groom like the interviewer is likely to be dressed and groomed, but just a bit better.

- **Give a firm handshake and maintain good eye contact.** If the employer offers his or her hand, give a firm (but not too firm) handshake as you smile. As ridiculous as it sounds, a little practice helps. Avoid staring, but do look at the interviewer when either of you is speaking. It will help you concentrate on what is being said and indicate to the employer that you are listening closely and have good social skills.

- **Act interested.** When you are sitting, lean slightly forward in your chair and keep your head up, looking directly at the interviewer. This stance helps you look interested and alert.

- **Eliminate annoying behaviors.** Try to eliminate any distracting movements or mannerisms. A woman in one of my workshops saw herself in a videotape constantly playing with her hair. Only then did she realize that she had this distracting behavior. Listen to yourself and you may notice that you say "aaahhh" or "ummmmm" frequently, or say "you know what I mean?" over and over, or use other repetitive words or phrases. You may hardly be aware of doing this, but do watch for it. Ask friends or family for help pinpointing these behaviors.

- **Pay attention to your voice.** If you are naturally soft-spoken, work on increasing your volume slightly. Listen to news announcers and other professional speakers who are good models for volume, speed, and voice tone. I, for example, have a fairly deep voice. I have learned to change my intonation while doing presentations so that everyone doesn't go to sleep. Your voice and delivery will improve as you gain experience and conduct more interviews.

- **Use the interviewer's formal name as often as possible.** Do this particularly in the early part of the interview and again when you are ending it. Do not call the interviewer by his or her first name unless the interviewer suggests otherwise.

- **Play the chitchat game for awhile.** Interviewers often comment on the weather, ask if you had trouble getting there, or make some other common opening. Be friendly and make a few appropriate comments. Do not push your way into the business of your visit too early because these informal openings are standard measures of your socialization skills. Smile. It's nonverbal, and people will respond more favorably to you if you smile at them.

- **Comment on something personal in the interviewer's office.** "I love your office! Did you decorate it yourself?" or "I noticed the sailboat. Do you sail?" or "Your office manager is great! How long has he been here?" The idea here is to express interest in something that interests the employer and encourage her or him to speak about it. This kind of interest is a compliment if your enthusiasm shows. This tactic can also provide you the opportunity to share something you have in common, so try to pick a topic you know something about.

- **Ask some opening questions.** As soon as you have completed the necessary pleasant chitchat, be prepared to guide the interview in the direction you wish it to go. This process can happen within a minute of your first greeting, but is more likely to take up to five minutes. See the section later in this chapter titled "Use Control Statements to Your Advantage" for details on how to do this.

2. Communicate Your Skills

If you have created a reasonably positive image of yourself so far, an interviewer will now be interested in the specifics of why they should consider hiring you. This back-and-forth conversation usually lasts from 15 to 45 minutes and many consider it to be the most important and most difficult task in the entire job search.

Fortunately, by reading this book, you will have several advantages over the average job seeker:

1. You will know what sort of job you want.
2. You will know what skills are required to do well in that job.
3. You will have those very skills.

The only thing you have to do is to communicate these three things by directly and completely answering the questions an employer asks you. Chapter 2 helps you recognize your skills and communicate them to an interviewer.

3. Use Control Statements to Your Advantage

A *control statement* is a statement you make that becomes the roadmap for where the conversation (interview) is going. Although you might think you are at the mercy of the interviewer, you do have some ability to set the direction of the interview from the chitchat to the focus you desire.

For example, you might say something direct, such as "I'd like to tell you about what I've done, what I enjoy doing, and why I think it would be a good match with your organization." Your control statement can come at the beginning of the interview if things seem fuzzy after the chitchat or any time in the interview when you feel the focus is shifting away from the points you want to make.

Here are some other control statements and questions to ask early in an interview:

- "How did you get started in this type of career?"
- "I'd like to know more about what your organization does. Would you mind telling me?"

- "I have a background in _____ and am interested in how I might be considered for a position in an organization such as yours."

- "I have three years of experience plus two years of training in the field of _____. I am actively looking for a job and know that you probably do not have openings now; but I would be interested in future openings. Perhaps if I told you a few things about myself, you could give me some idea of whether you would be interested in me."

4. Answer Problem Questions Well

All employers try to uncover problems or limitations you might bring to their job. Yet according to employers in Northwestern University's Endicott Report, about 80 percent of all job seekers cannot provide a good answer to one or more problem interview questions. Everyone has a problem of some sort, and the employer will try to find yours. Expect it. Suppose that you have been out of work for three months. That could be seen as a problem, unless you can provide a good reason for it. Chapter 5 gives more guidance on answering problem questions and other key questions you might be asked.

5. Ask Good Questions

Many employers ask at some point in the interview whether you have any questions. How you respond affects their evaluation of you. So be prepared to ask insightful questions about the organization. Good topics to touch on include the following:

- The competitive environment in which the organization operates

- Executive management styles

- What obstacles the organization anticipates in meeting its goals

- How the organization's goals have changed over the past three to five years

Generally, asking about pay, benefits, or other similar topics at this time is unwise. The reason is that doing so tends to make you seem more interested in what the organization can do for you, rather than in what you can do for it. Having no questions at all makes you appear passive or disinterested, rather than curious and interested.

6. Help Employers Know Why They Should Hire You

Even if the interviewer never directly says it, the question in his or her mind is always "Why should I hire you over someone else?" The best response to this question provides advantages to the employer, not to you. A good response provides proof that you can help an employer make more money by improving efficiency, reducing costs, increasing sales, or solving problems (by coming to work on time, improving customer service, organizing one or more operations, offering knowledge of a particular software or computer system, or a variety of other things). See chapter 4 for guidance on answering this all-important question.

7. Close the Interview Properly

As the interview comes to an end, remember these few things:

- **Don't let the interview last too long.** Most interviews last 30 to 60 minutes. Unless the interviewer asks otherwise, plan on staying no longer than an hour. Watch for hints from interviewers, such as looking at a watch or rustling papers, that indicate that they are ready to end the interview.

- **Summarize the key points of the interview.** Use your judgment here and keep it short! Review the major issues that came up in the interview with the employer. You can skip this step if time is short.

- **If a problem came up, repeat your resolution of it.** Whatever you think that particular interviewer may see as a reason not to hire you, bring it up again and present your reasons why you don't see it as a problem. If you are not sure what the interviewer is thinking, be direct and ask, "Is there anything about me that concerns you or might keep you from hiring me?" Whatever comes up, do as well as you can in responding to it.

- **Review your strengths for this job.** Take this opportunity to present the skills you possess that relate to this particular job one more time. Emphasize your key strengths only and keep your statements brief.

- **If you want the job, ask for it.** If you want the job, say so and explain why. Employers are more willing to hire someone they know is excited about the job, so let them know if you are. Ask when you can start. This question may not always be appropriate, but if it is, do it.

The Call-Back Close

This interview-closing approach requires some courage, but it does work. Practice it a few times and use it in your early interviews to get more comfortable with it.

1. **Thank the interviewer by name.** While shaking their hand, say, "Thank you (Mr. or Mrs. or Ms. _____) for your time today."

2. **Express interest.** Depending on the situation, express your interest in the job, organization, service, or product by saying, "I'm very interested in the ideas we went over today," or "I'm very interested in your organization. It seems to be an exciting place to work." Or, if a job opening exists and you want it, confidently say, "I am definitely interested in this position."

3. **Mention your busy schedule.** Say "I'm busy for the next few days, but..."

4. **Arrange a reason and a time to call back.** Your objective is to leave a reason for you to get back in touch and to arrange for a specific day and time to do so. For example, say, "I'm sure I'll have questions. When would be the best time for me to get back with you?" Notice that I said "When" rather than "Is it OK to..." because asking *when* does not easily allow a "no" response. Get a specific day and a best time to call.

5. **Say good-bye.**

8. Follow Up After the Interview

The interview has ended, you made it home, and now you just sit back and wait, right? Wrong. Effective follow-up actions can make a big difference in getting a job offer over more qualified applicants.

As I say throughout this book, following up can make the difference between being unemployed or underemployed and getting the job you want fast. See chapter 7 for more details on effective follow-up by phone, e-mail, and regular mail.

The Three-Step Process for Answering Most Interview Questions

There are thousands of questions that you could be asked in an interview, and there is no way you can memorize a "correct" response for each one—especially not the night before the interview. Interviews just aren't like that because they are often conversational and informal. The unexpected often happens. For these reasons, developing an *approach* to answering an interview question is far more important than memorizing a canned response.

I have developed a technique called the Three-Step Process that you can use to fashion an effective answer to most interview questions:

1. **Understand what is really being asked.** Most questions relate to your adaptive skills and personality. These questions include "Can we depend on you?"; "Are you easy to get along with?"; and "Are you a good worker?" The question may also relate to whether you have the experience and training to do the job if you are hired.

2. **Answer the question briefly in a non-damaging way.** A good response to a question should acknowledge the facts of your situation and present them as an advantage rather than a disadvantage.

3. **Answer the real question by presenting your related skills.** An effective response to any interview question should answer the question in a direct way that also presents your ability to do the job well.

To show you how to use the Three-Step Process, let's use it to answer a specific question:

> **Question:** "We were looking for someone with more experience in this field than you seem to have. Why should we consider you over others with better credentials?"

The following sections show how one person might construct an answer to this question using the Three-Step Process.

Step 1: Understand What Is Really Being Asked

This question is often asked in a less direct way, but it is a frequent concern of employers. To answer it, you must remember that employers often hire people who present themselves well in an interview over those with better credentials. Your best shot is to emphasize whatever personal strengths you have that could offer an advantage to an employer. The person wants to know whether you have anything going for you that can help you compete with a more experienced worker.

Well, do you? Are you a hard worker? Do you learn fast? Have you had intensive training or hands-on experience? Do you have skills from other activities that can transfer to this job? Knowing in advance what skills you have to offer is essential to answering this question.

Step 2: Answer the Question Briefly in a Non-Damaging Way

For example, the following response answers the question without hurting the person's chances of getting the job:

> "I'm sure there are people who have more years of experience or better credentials. I do, however, have four years of combined training and hands-on experience using the latest methods and techniques. Because my training is recent, I am open to new ideas and am used to working hard and learning quickly."

Step 3: Answer the Real Question by Presenting Your Related Skills

Although the previous response answers the question in an appropriate and brief way, you might continue with additional details that emphasize key skills needed for the job:

> "As you know, I held down a full-time job and family responsibilities while going to school. During those two years, I had an excellent attendance record both at work and school, missing only one day in two years. I also received two merit increases in salary, and my grades were in the top 25 percent of my class. In order to do all this, I had to learn to organize my time and set priorities. I worked hard to prepare myself in this new career area and am willing to keep working to establish myself. The position you have available is what I am prepared to do. I am willing to work harder than the next person because I have the desire to keep learning and to do an outstanding job. With my education complete, I can now turn my full attention to this job."

This response presents the skills necessary to do well in any job. This job seeker sounds dependable. She also gave examples of situations where she had used the required skills in other settings. It is a good response.

Chapter 4 shows you how to use the Three-Step Process to provide thorough answers to 10 interview questions that, in one form or another, are asked in most interviews. If you can answer those questions well, you should be prepared to answer almost any question. Chapter 5 provides answers to a wide variety of more-specific interview questions you may be asked.

The Prove-It Technique

The Three-Step Process is important for understanding that the interview question being asked is often an attempt to discover underlying information. You can provide that information in an effective way by using the four-step Prove-It Technique:

1. **Present a concrete example:** People relate to and remember stories. Saying you have a skill is not nearly as powerful as describing a situation where you used that skill. The example should include enough details to make sense of the who, what, where, when, and why.

2. **Quantify:** Whenever possible, use numbers to provide a basis for what you did. For example, give the number of customers served, the percent you exceeded quotas, dollar amounts you were responsible for, or the number of new accounts you generated.

3. **Emphasize results:** Providing some data regarding the positive results you obtained is important. For example, you could state that sales increased by 3 percent over the previous year or profits went up 50 percent. Use numbers to quantify your results.

4. **Link it up:** Although the connection between your example and doing the job well may seem obvious to you, make sure it is clear to the employer. A simple statement is often enough to accomplish this.

If you do a thorough job of completing the activities in chapter 2, providing proof supporting the skills you discuss in an interview should be fairly easy.

Key Points: Chapter 1

- No matter what type of interview you face, you must stay focused on conveying the job skills you have in order to be successful.

- There are several things you should do to have a successful interview, including make a good impression, answer tough questions well, and follow up after the interview.

- By using the Three-Step Process, you can handle any interview question. First make sure you understand what is really being asked, then briefly respond to the question in a non-damaging way, and finally present your related job skills to answer the true question.

- To support the skills you discuss in interviews, you can use the Prove-It Technique. To use the Prove-It Technique, you give examples for, quantify, and list results for each job skill you present. You also must be able to relate your job skills to the position you are applying for.

Chapter 2

Knowing Yourself and What You Can Do

K nowing what you are good at is an essential part of doing well in a job interview. It is also important in other ways. For example, unless you use the skills that you enjoy using and are good at, you are unlikely to be fully satisfied in your job.

Most people are not good at recognizing and listing the skills they have. I can tell you this based on many years of working with groups of job seekers. When asked, few people can quickly tell me what they are good at, and fewer still can quickly present the specific skills that are needed to succeed in the job they want.

Many employers also note that most job seekers don't present their skills effectively. According to one survey of employers, more than 90 percent of the people they interview cannot adequately define the skills they have that support their ability to do the job. Many job seekers have the necessary skills, but they can't communicate that fact. This chapter is designed to help you fix that problem.

Learn the Three Types of Skills

Simple skills such as closing your fingers to grip a pen (which is not simple at all if you consider the miracle of complex neuromuscular interactions that sophisticated robots can only approximate) are building blocks for more complex skills, such as writing a sentence, and even more complex skills, such as writing a book. Even though you have hundreds of skills, some will be more important to an employer than others. Some will be far more important to you in deciding what sort of job you want. To simplify the task of skill identification, I have found it useful to think of skills in the three major categories: adaptive skills, transferable skills, and job-related skills.

Adaptive Skills/Personality Traits

You probably take for granted the many skills you use every day to survive and function. I call these skills *adaptive* or *self-management skills* because they allow you to adapt or adjust to a variety of situations. Some of them could be considered part of your basic personality. Such skills, which are highly valued by employers, include getting to work on time, honesty, enthusiasm, and getting along with others.

The Skills Employers Want

To illustrate that employers value adaptive and transferable skills very highly, I have included the results of a survey of employers here. This information comes from a study of employers called Workplace Basics—The Skills Employers Want. The study was conducted jointly by the U.S. Department of Labor and the American Association of Counseling and Development.

It turns out that most of the skills employers want are either adaptive or transferable skills. Of course, specific job-related skills remain important, but basic skills form an essential foundation for success on the job. Here are the top skills employers identified:

1. Learning to learn
2. Basic academic skills in reading, writing, and computation
3. Good communication skills, including listening and speaking
4. Creative thinking and problem solving
5. Self-esteem, motivation, and goal setting
6. Personal and career development skills
7. Interpersonal/negotiation skills and teamwork
8. Organizational effectiveness and leadership

What is most interesting is that most of these skills are not formally taught in school. Yet these so-called soft skills are those that employers value most. Of course, job-related skills are also important (an accountant still needs to know accounting skills), but the adaptive and transferable skills are the ones that allow you to succeed in any job.

Again, this study shows the importance of being aware of your skills and using them well in career planning. If you have any weaknesses in one or more of the skills that were listed, consider improvements. Always remember to turn your weaknesses into strengths. For example, if you don't have a specific skill that's required for a job, let the employer know that you don't, but add that you are eager to learn and you are a quick study. This comment shows the employer that you are not afraid of learning new skills and that you are confident in your abilities. Furthermore, if you are already strong in one or more of the top skills employers want, look for opportunities to develop and use them in your work or to present them clearly in your next interview.

Transferable Skills

Transferable skills are general skills that can be useful in a variety of jobs. For example, writing clearly, good language skills, or the ability to organize and prioritize tasks are desirable skills in many jobs. These skills are called *transferable skills* because they can be transferred from one job—or even one career—to another.

Job-Related Skills

Job-related skills are the skills people typically think of first when asked, "Do you have any skills?" They are related to a particular job or type of job. An auto mechanic, for example, needs to know how to tune engines and repair brakes. Other jobs also have job-related skills required for that job in addition to the adaptive and transferable skills needed to succeed in almost any job.

This system of dividing skills into three categories is not perfect. Some things, such as being trustworthy, dependable, or well-organized, are not skills as much as they are personality traits that can be acquired. There is also some overlap between the three skills categories. For example, a skill such as being organized might be considered either adaptive or transferable.

Identify Your Skills

Because being aware of your skills is so important, I include a series of checklists and other activities in this chapter to help you identify your key skills. Recognizing these skills is important so that you can select jobs that you will do well in. Skills are also important to recognize and emphasize in a job interview. Developing a skills language can also be very helpful to you in writing resumes and conducting your job search. To begin, answer the question in the box.

WHAT MAKES YOU A GOOD WORKER?

On the following lines, list three things about yourself that you think make you a good worker. Take your time. Think about what an employer might like about you or the way you work.

1. _____

2. _____

3. _____

The skills you just wrote down may be among the most important things that an employer will want to know about you. Most (but not all) people write adaptive skills when asked this question. Whatever you wrote, these skills are often very important to mention in the interview. In fact, presenting these skills well will often allow a less experienced job seeker to get the job over someone with better credentials. Most employers are willing to train a person who lacks some job-related skills, but has the adaptive skills that the employer is looking for. Some employers even prefer job seekers with better adaptive skills than job-related skills because they are more malleable and not set in their ways.

Identify Your Adaptive Skills and Personality Traits

I have created a list of adaptive skills that tend to be important to employers. The ones listed as "The Minimum" are those that most employers consider essential for job survival, and many employers will not hire someone who has problems in these areas.

Look over the list and put a check mark next to each adaptive skill that you possess. Put a second check mark next to those skills that are particularly important for you to use or include in your next job.

ADAPTIVE SKILLS WORKSHEET

The Minimum

___ Have good attendance   ___ Meet deadlines

___ Am honest   ___ Get along with supervisor

___ Arrive on time   ___ Get along with coworkers

___ Follow instructions   ___ Am hardworking, productive

Other Adaptive Skills

___ Coordinating	___ Intuitive	___ Problem-solving
___ Results-oriented	___ Decisive	___ Team player
___ Mentoring	___ Working well with people from diverse backgrounds	___ Multitasking
___ Friendly	___ Discreet	___ Patient
___ Ambitious	___ Quick-learning	___ Spontaneous
___ Good-natured	___ Eager	___ Persistent
___ Assertive	___ Loyal	___ Steady
___ Helpful	___ Efficient	___ Physically strong
___ Capable	___ Mature	___ Tactful
___ Humble	___ Energetic	___ Practical
___ Cheerful	___ Methodical	___ Proud of work
___ Imaginative	___ Enthusiastic	___ Competent
___ Modest	___ Reliable	___ Independent
___ Expressive	___ Tenacious	___ Well-organized
___ Motivated	___ Resourceful	___ Industrious
___ Flexible	___ Thrifty	___ Natural
___ Responsible	___ Conscientious	___ Formal

___ Trustworthy	___ Informal	___ Open-minded
___ Self-confident	___ Creative	___ Optimistic
___ Versatile	___ Intelligent	___ Sincere
___ Humorous	___ Dependable	___ Original

Other Similar Adaptive Skills You Have

Add any adaptive skills that were not listed but that you think are important to include:

_____

_____

_____

_____

_____

_____

Your Top Adaptive Skills

Carefully review the checklist you just completed and select the three adaptive skills you feel are most important for you to tell an employer about or that you most want to use in your next job. These three skills are *extremely* important to present to an employer in an interview.

1. _____

2. _____

3. _____

Identify Your Transferable Skills

Over the years, I have assembled a list of transferable skills that are important in a wide variety of jobs. In the checklist that follows, the skills listed as "Key Transferable Skills" are those that I consider to be most important for success on the job. These skills are also those that are often required in jobs with more responsibility and higher pay, so you should emphasize these skills if you have them.

The remaining transferable skills are grouped into categories that may be helpful to you. Go ahead and check each skill you are strong in, and then double-check the skills you want to use in your next job. When you are finished, you should have checked 10 to 20 skills at least once.

TRANSFERABLE SKILLS CHECKLIST

Key Transferable Skills

____ Meeting deadlines

____ Planning

____ Speaking in public

____ Controlling budgets

____ Meeting the public

____ Negotiating

____ Instructing others

____ Organizing or managing projects

____ Solving problems

____ Managing money or budgets

____ Managing people

____ Supervising others

____ Increasing sales or efficiency

____ Accepting responsibility

____ Writing

____ Using computer or other technology appropriate for my job objective

Other Transferable Skills

____ Drive or operate vehicles

____ Build, observe, or inspect things

____ Assemble or make things

____ Construct or repair buildings

Dealing with Data

____ Analyze data or facts

____ Investigate

____ Audit records

____ Keep financial records

____ Negotiate

____ Compare, inspect, or record facts

____ Count, observe, compile

____ Research

____ Budget

____ Locate answers or information

____ Calculate, compute

____ Manage money

____ Classify data

____ Pay attention to detail

____ Use technology to analyze data

____ Evaluate

____ Take inventory

____ Synthesize

Working with People

____ Administer

____ Patient

____ Care for others

____ Persuade

____ Confront others

____ Teach

____ Interview others

____ Be tolerant

____ Negotiate

____ Be pleasant

____ Counsel people

____ Be sensitive

____ Demonstrate

____ Socialize

____ Be tough

____ Listen

____ Trust

____ Be diplomatic

____ Supervise

____ Help others

____ Be tactful

____ Have insight

____ Understand

____ Be outgoing

____ Be kind

Using Words, Ideas

____ Be articulate

____ Design

____ Speak in public

____ Remember information

____ Write clearly

____ Research

____ Create new ideas

____ Correspond with others

____ Invent

____ Communicate verbally

____ Edit

____ Think logically

____ Be ingenious

(continued)

(continued)

Leadership

____ Arrange social functions	____ Direct others
____ Motivate people	____ Exercise self-control
____ Be competitive	____ Explain things to others
____ Negotiate agreements	____ Motivate yourself
____ Make decisions	____ Get results
____ Plan	____ Solve problems
____ Delegate	____ Mediate problems
____ Run meetings	____ Take risks

Creative, Artistic

____ Be artistic	____ Perform, act	____ Express yourself
____ Appreciate music	____ Draw	____ Dance
____ Present artistic ideas	____ Play instruments	

Other Similar Transferable Skills You Have

Add any transferable skills that were not listed but that you think are important to include:

_____

_____

_____

_____

_____

Your Top Transferable Skills

Select the five top transferable skills you have that you want to use in your next job and list them below:

1. _____

2. _____

3. _____

4. _____

5. _____

Identify Your Job-Related Skills

Many jobs require skills that are specific to that occupation. An airline pilot obviously needs to know how to fly an airplane; thankfully, having good adaptive and transferable skills would not be enough to be considered for that job.

Job-related skills may have been gained in a variety of ways including education, training, work, hobbies, or other life experiences. As you complete the various worksheets that follow, keep in mind that you are looking for skills and accomplishments. Pay special attention to those experiences and accomplishments that you really enjoyed; these experiences often demonstrate skills that you should try to use in your next job. When possible, quantify your activities or their results with numbers. Employers can relate more easily to percentages, raw numbers, and ratios than to quality terms such as *more, many, greater, less, fewer,* and so on. For example, saying "presented to groups as large as 200 people" has more impact than "did many presentations."

EDUCATION AND TRAINING WORKSHEET

We spend many years in school and learn more lessons there than you might at first realize. For example, in our early years of schooling we acquire basic skills that are important in most jobs: getting along with others, reading instructions, and accepting supervision. Later, courses become more specialized and relevant to potential careers.

This worksheet helps you review all your education and training experiences, even those that may have occurred years ago. Some courses may seem more important to certain careers than others. But keep in mind that even the courses that don't seem to support a particular career choice can be an important source of skills.

Elementary Grades

Although few employers will ask you about these years, jot down any highlights of things you felt particularly good about; doing so may help you identify important interests and directions to consider for the future. For example, note the following:

- Subjects you did well in that might relate to the job you want
- Extracurricular activities/hobbies/leisure activities
- Accomplishments/things you did well (in or out of school)

High School Experiences

These experiences will be more important for a recent graduate and less so for those with college, work, or other life experiences. But, whatever your situation, what you did during these years can give you important clues to use in your career planning and job search.

Name of school(s)/years attended:

_____

Subjects you did well in or that might relate to the job you want:

_____

_____

_____

Extracurricular activities/hobbies/leisure activities:

_____

_____

_____

Accomplishments/things you did well (in or out of school):

_____

_____

_____

_____

_____

_____

Postsecondary or College Experiences

If you attended or graduated from a two- or four-year college or took college classes, what you learned and did during this time will often be of interest to an employer. If you are a new graduate, these experiences can be particularly important because you have less work experience to present. Emphasize here those things that directly support your ability to do the job. For example, working your way through school shows that you are hardworking. If you took courses that specifically support your job, you can include details on these as well.

Name of school(s)/years attended:

_____

_____

Major:

_____

Courses related to job objective:

_____

_____

(continued)

(continued)

_____

_____

Extracurricular activities/hobbies/leisure activities:

_____

_____

_____

_____

Accomplishments/things you did well (in or out of school):

_____

_____

_____

_____

_____

Specific things you learned or can do that relate to the job you want:

_____

_____

_____

_____

Additional Training and Education

There are many formal and informal ways to learn, and some of the most important things are often learned outside of the classroom. Use this worksheet to list any additional training or education that might relate to the job you want. Include military training, on-the-job training, workshops, or any other formal or informal training you have had. You can also include any substantial learning you obtained through a hobby, family activities, online research, or similar informal source.

Names of courses or programs/dates taken/any certificates or credentials earned:

_____

_____

_____

_____

_____

_____

Specific things you learned or can do that relate to the job you want:

_____

_____

_____

_____

_____

_____

JOB AND VOLUNTEER HISTORY WORKSHEET

Use this worksheet to list each major job you have held and the information related to each. Begin with your most recent job, followed by previous ones.

Include military experience and unpaid volunteer work here, too. Both are work and are particularly important if you do not have much paid civilian work experience. Create additional sheets to cover all of your significant jobs or unpaid experiences as needed. If you have been promoted, consider handling the new position as a separate job from the original position.

Whenever possible, provide numbers to support what you did: number of people served over one or more years; number of transactions processed; percentage of sales increase; total inventory value you were

(continued)

(continued)

responsible for; payroll of the staff you supervised; total budget you were responsible for; and other specific data. As much as possible, mention results using numbers, as well.

Job #1

Name of organization: _____

Address: _____

Job title(s): _____

Employed from: _____ to: _____

Computers, software, or other machinery or equipment you used:

_____

_____

_____

Data, information, or reports you created or used:

_____

_____

_____

People-oriented duties or responsibilities to coworkers, customers, others:

_____

_____

_____

_____

_____

Services you provided or products you produced:

_____

_____

_____

_____

_____

Reasons for promotions or salary increases, if any:

_____

_____

_____

_____

_____

Details on anything you did to help the organization, such as increase productivity, improve procedures or processes, simplify or reorganize job duties, decrease costs, increase profits, improve working conditions, reduce turnover, or other improvements. Quantify results when possible; use statements such as, "Increased order processing by 50 percent, with no increase in staff costs."

_____

_____

_____

Specific things you learned or can do that relate to the job you want:

_____

_____

_____

_____

What would your supervisor say about you?

_____

_____

_____

_____

(continued)

(continued)

Supervisor's name: _____

Phone number: _____ E-mail address: _____

Job #2

Name of organization: _____

Address: _____

Job title(s): _____

Employed from: _____ to: _____

Computers, software, or other machinery or equipment you used:

_____

_____

_____

Data, information, or reports you created or used:

_____

_____

_____

People-oriented duties or responsibilities to coworkers, customers, others:

_____

_____

_____

_____

_____

Services you provided or products you produced:

_____

_____

_____

_____

_____

Reasons for promotions or salary increases, if any:

_____

_____

Details on anything you did to help the organization, such as increase productivity, improve procedures or processes, simplify or reorganize job duties, decrease costs, increase profits, improve working conditions, reduce turnover, or other improvements. Quantify results when possible.

_____

_____

_____

Specific things you learned or can do that relate to the job you want:

_____

_____

_____

_____

_____

What would your supervisor say about you?

_____

_____

_____

_____

_____

Supervisor's name: _____

Phone number: _____ E-mail address: _____

(continued)

(continued)

Job #3

Name of organization: _____

Address: _____

Job title(s): _____

Employed from: _____ to: _____

Computers, software, or other machinery or equipment you used:

_____

_____

_____

Data, information, or reports you created or used:

_____

_____

_____

People-oriented duties or responsibilities to coworkers, customers, others:

_____

_____

_____

_____

_____

Services you provided or products you produced:

_____

_____

_____

_____

_____

Reasons for promotions or salary increases, if any:

_____

_____

_____

_____

Details on anything you did to help the organization, such as increase productivity, improve procedures or processes, simplify or reorganize job duties, decrease costs, increase profits, improve working conditions, reduce turnover, or other improvements. Quantify results when possible.

_____

_____

_____

Specific things you learned or can do that relate to the job you want:

_____

_____

_____

_____

_____

What would your supervisor say about you?

_____

_____

_____

_____

_____

Supervisor's name: _____

Phone number: _____ E-mail address: _____

(continued)

(continued)

Job #4

Name of organization: _____

Address: _____

Job title(s): _____

Employed from: _____ to: _____

Computers, software, or other machinery or equipment you used:

_____

_____

_____

Data, information, or reports you created or used:

_____

_____

_____

People-oriented duties or responsibilities to coworkers, customers, others:

_____

_____

_____

_____

_____

Services you provided or products you produced:

_____

_____

_____

_____

_____

Reasons for promotions or salary increases, if any:

_____

_____

_____

_____

_____

Details on anything you did to help the organization, such as increase productivity, improve procedures or processes, simplify or reorganize job duties, decrease costs, increase profits, improve working conditions, reduce turnover, or other improvements. Quantify results when possible.

_____

_____

_____

Specific things you learned or can do that relate to the job you want:

_____

_____

_____

_____

_____

What would your supervisor say about you?

_____

_____

_____

_____

_____

Supervisor's name: _____

Phone number: _____ E-mail address: _____

OTHER LIFE EXPERIENCES WORKSHEET

Many people overlook informal life experiences as being important
sources of learning or accomplishment. This worksheet is here to
encourage you to think about any hobbies or interests you have had:
family responsibilities, recreational activities, travel, or any other
experiences in your life where you feel some sense of accomplishment. Write any experiences that seem particularly meaningful to you
below, and name the key skills you think were involved.

Situation 1:

Describe situation and skills used:

_____

_____

_____

_____

_____

Specific things you learned or can do that relate to the job you want:

_____

_____

_____

_____

Situation 2:

Describe situation and skills used:

_____

_____

_____

_____

_____

Specific things you learned or can do that relate to the job you want:

_____

_____

_____

_____

_____

Situation 3:

Describe situation and skills used:

_____

_____

_____

_____

_____

Specific things you learned or can do that relate to the job you want:

_____

_____

_____

_____

Your Top Job-Related Skills

Of all the job-related skills you have, list the five most important ones you think an employer should know about below:

1. _____

2. _____

3. _____

4. _____

5. _____

Key Points: Chapter 2

- Knowing your skills is essential for answering most interview questions. Once you develop your "skills language," you can use it to help identify jobs that match these skills, write better resumes, and find a job that more closely matches what you are good at and enjoy doing.

- Adaptive skills such as having good work habits and working well with others are important to employers.

- Transferable skills, which include writing, managing people, and analyzing data, are useful in many different careers. Be sure to emphasize your relevant transferable skills in interviews.

- Job-related skills are those skills you have learned through education, training, and job experience. When you discuss these skills in an interview, provide as many numbers, examples, and results as you can.

Chapter 3

Researching the Industry, Company, Job, and Interviewer

Employers don't have to hesitate when asked what they see as the number one problem with job candidates: a complete lack of preparation. True, a good many people are well-prepared to speak about themselves and their accomplishments, but they should have some knowledge about the job, the organization, and the interviewer as well.

Unfortunately, gaining that knowledge requires research, and many people resist doing it. As a result, many end up treating job information research as they did their high school term papers: They slap it together and hope for the best or avoid doing it completely. This lack of preparation often shows in the interview. This chapter takes the mystery out of research by pointing out where to turn, what to look for, and how to have fun doing it.

Find Good Information About the Industry

The industry information you gather will be invaluable to you at the latter stages of the interview process. Knowing that there are only 9,000 available certified property managers and 250,000 real estate firms needing agents, for example, allows you to present yourself as among the top 3 percent in the field—an excellent bargaining chip during the interview and at the salary negotiation table. (See chapter 8 for more on negotiating salary.)

Let's say that you have an interview tomorrow in a hospital. Even if you hope to work in a nonmedical area such as accounting, you will do better in the interview if you know something about the health care industry. The following two resources can help you find information about any industry in which you might be interested in working.

Career Guide to Industries

This book, published by the U.S. Department of Labor, is of particular value to job seekers. It provides helpful descriptions for more than 40 major industries, which cover about 75 percent of all jobs. The *Career Guide to Industries* is easy to read and provides information that can help you present yourself well in an interview.

Each description includes an overview of the industry, types of jobs it offers, employment projections, earnings possible, training required, working conditions, advancement opportunities, industry trends, sources of additional information, and more. You can find the *Career Guide to Industries* in your local library or bookstore. You can also access its contents online at stats.bls.gov/oco/cg/home.htm.

Hoover's Online

This site (www.hoovers.com) is the place to go online to find anything you need to know about industries and employers. You can search for information by company name, industry type, stock ticker, executives' names, and more. Basic information is free. For different subscription levels, you can get more details.

Other Sources of Industry Information

A good library has lots of information on industries. Industry trade magazines such as *Advertising Age, Automotive News, Hotel and Motel Management, Modern Healthcare,* and *Supermarket News* are full of articles detailing trends and problems in their particular niches. Grab the last six months' issues and settle down for some interesting reading.

While you have these publications in hand, photocopy and highlight facts that boost your position in that industry, and scribble in the margins some questions you'd like your prospective employer to answer. And always flip to the classifieds section—no use wasting a perfectly good chance to find a job lead!

Next, grab the library's current copy of the *Encyclopedia of Associations.* Don't let its name intimidate you—it is a gold mine of associations listed by categories. Each entry gives the contact information, mission statement,

> **Tip:** *Many trade magazines also maintain Web sites where you can go and browse information. You can find lists of many of these sites at dir.yahoo.com/ business_and_economy/ business_to_business/ news_and_media/ magazines/ trade_magazines/.*

newsletters, and conventions for that group. Pick the ones in your industry category that closely match your situation and give them a call or check out their Web sites. They will most likely send you copies of a recent newsletter or journal and provide other information.

Get More Information on the Careers That Interest You Most

You probably know what sort of job you will seek. That certitude may come as the result of past training, education, work experience, or other reasons. If this is your situation, you may be thinking that you already know about the jobs you want and don't need to learn more about them. But learning more about the jobs you're interested in is a good idea, for several reasons. By researching various options, you can do the following:

- **Increase opportunities in your job search by identifying a wider range of job targets.** There are thousands of specialized job titles, and, if you don't do some research, you are almost certain to overlook a number of them that would fit your needs very well. Looking up a few job titles is a start, but reviewing all jobs within clusters of similar jobs is likely to help you identify jobs you don't know much about—but which would be good ones for you to consider.

- **Improve your interview skills.** Sure, you may think you know what's involved in a particular job, but you still need to prepare for an interview. Most people with substantial education, training, and work experience in a particular job do not do a good job of presenting their skills for that job in the interview. People who do their homework by carefully reading a job description and then mentioning key skills that job requires in an interview often get job offers over those with better credentials. Why? They do a more convincing job in the interview by making it easier for employers to understand why they should hire this job seeker over another.

- **Write a better resume.** Knowing the specific skills a job requires allows you to focus on those skills in your resume.

Out of the hundreds of sources of career information, an important few will give you most of what you need. I've listed these few primary resources here, along with information on where to find them.

The Guide for Occupational Exploration

After extensive research, the U.S. Department of Labor developed an easy-to-use system that organized all jobs by interest. For example, if you are interested in artistic activities, this system would allow you to identify the many jobs related to this area. This interest-based system is presented in a book titled the *Guide for Occupational Exploration (GOE)* and is used in a variety of print and computer career information systems.

The current edition of the *GOE* organizes all jobs into 14 major interest areas. These areas are further divided into more specific groupings (called *work groups*) of related jobs. The GOE system is easy to understand and use, yet it is powerful enough to allow thousands of job titles to be organized into its various work groups.

The *GOE* allows you to quickly identify groups of jobs that are most closely related to what you want to do. All along the way, from major interest areas to the more specific work groups, helpful information is provided related to each group of jobs.

The Occupational Outlook Handbook

I consider the *Occupational Outlook Handbook* (which I will hereafter refer to as the *OOH*) to be one of the most helpful books on career information available. I urge you either to buy one or arrange for frequent access to it throughout your job search because it is useful in a variety of ways.

The *OOH* provides descriptions for about 280 of America's most popular jobs, organized within clusters of related jobs. Although that number may not sound like many jobs, about 87 percent of the workforce works in these 280 jobs.

The *OOH* is updated every two years by the U.S. Department of Labor and provides the latest information on salaries, growth projections, related jobs, required skills, education or training needed, working conditions, and many other details. Each job is described in a readable, interesting format.

You can use the *OOH* in many ways. Here are some suggestions:

- **Identify the skills needed in the job you want.** Look up a job that interests you, and the *OOH* tells you the transferable and job-related skills it requires. Assuming that you have these skills, you can then emphasize them in interviews.

- **Find skills from previous jobs to support your present objective.** Look up *OOH* descriptions for jobs you have had in the past. A careful read will help you identify skills that can be transferred and used in the new job. Even "minor" jobs can be valuable in this way. For example, if you waited on tables while going to school, you would discover that this job requires the ability to work under pressure, deal with customers, and work quickly. If you are now looking for a job as an accountant, you can see how transferable skills used in an apparently unrelated past job can support your ability to do another job. If you are changing careers or don't have much work experience related to the job you want, describing your transferable skills can be very important.

- **Identify related job targets.** Each major job description in the *OOH* lists other jobs that are closely related. The description also provides information on positions that the job might lead to through promotion or experience. Because the jobs are listed within clusters of similar jobs, you can easily browse descriptions of related jobs you may have overlooked. All of this detail gives you options to consider in your job search.

- **Find out the typical salary range, trends, and other details.** The *OOH* helps you know what pay range to expect and which trends are affecting the job. Note that local pay averages and other details can differ significantly from the national information provided in the *OOH*.

- **Get more specific information on a particular job and related jobs.** If a job interests you, learning more about it is important. Each *OOH* job description provides helpful sources, including a cross-reference to the O*NET career information (see next section), related professional associations, Internet sites, and other sources.

> **Tip:** *Most libraries have the* Occupational Outlook Handbook, *but you probably won't be able to take it home. Another book titled* America's Top 300 Jobs *provides the same information (plus my job search tips) and is often available for circulation. You can order either book through JIST or most bookstores. You should use these books as reference tools frequently during your job search and after. You can also access the OOH information online at www.careeroink.com or at www.bls.gov/oco.*

The Occupational Information Network (O*NET)

The U.S. Department of Labor maintains an up-to-date computer data-base of occupational information. Called the O*NET, it provides detailed information for almost 1,200 jobs. Although the *OOH* is more useful for most situations, the O*NET describes many more jobs (and more special-ized jobs) and provides more details on each one.

The O*NET database offers basic descriptions for each of its jobs, plus 450 additional data elements for each job. Keep in mind that the O*NET is a complex database and much of the detailed information it provides is not of much use for most job seekers. Fortunately, career counselors have developed more helpful versions of the O*NET database. A book version published by JIST and titled the *O*NET Dictionary of Occupational Titles* was designed to provide the O*NET information of greatest value to most job seekers in an easy-to-use book format.

The job descriptions in this book are presented in an easy-to-use format that is packed with information, including the following:

- **O*NET Number:** The number to use to cross-reference other systems.

- **O*NET Occupational Title:** The job title that is most often used for this job.

- **Employed:** The total number of people who work in that job.

- **Annual Earnings:** The average annual earnings for people employed in the job.

- **Annual Job Openings:** The number of job openings per year project-ed for the job.

- **O*NET Occupational Description:** A brief but useful review of what a person working in that job would typically do.

- **GOE Information:** The Interest Area and Work Group for this job in the *Guide for Occupational Exploration*.

- **Personality Type:** What personality type the job best fits with.

- **Work Values:** Any of the job's 21 work values with high scores in the O*NET database.

- **Skills:** A variety of skills needed to perform at above-average levels in each job. Depending on the occupation, some of these skills are quite complex; others are relatively basic.

- **General Work Activities:** The general types of work activities needed to perform the job described.

- **Physical Work Conditions:** Information on work hazards, environment, required physical strength, and other measures.

- **Knowledge:** Areas of knowledge required to successfully perform in the occupation described. The knowledge may have been obtained from formal or informal sources, including high school or college courses or majors, training programs, self-employment, military, paid or volunteer work experience, or other life experience.

- **Job Characteristics:** Includes several types of information such as interacting with others, mental processes, role relationships, communication methods, responsibility for others, and many more.

- **Experience:** Lists the work or other experience the job requires.

- **Job Preparation:** Provides specific information on the training or education level the job requires.

- **Instructional Programs:** A cross-reference to a system that provides information on the type of training and education typically required for entry into the occupation.

- **Related *Dictionary of Occupational Titles* Jobs:** Related job titles from the *DOT,* a standard reference book that describes more than 12,000 jobs.

The complete set of O*NET information is available on the Internet at online.onetcenter.org/. I recommend, however, that you use the *O*NET Dictionary of Occupational Titles* book because it was designed for career exploration and job seeking.

CareerOINK

JIST operates the Web site at www.careerOINK.com to provide a variety of helpful career information resources, including the following:

- Lookup of jobs in *GOE* interest areas and groups

- Self-assessment tools

- Sample resumes

- Quick lookup of the more than 14,000 job descriptions from the *OOH*, O*NET, and *DOT*

- Military-to-civilian job cross-references and many other free resources

Know About the Specific Company, Job, and Interviewer

You should evaluate employers just as carefully as they evaluate you. Doing research on an employer is especially important if you plan on interviewing with an organization that particularly interests you.

The best employer information comes from people who work (or used to work) there. These people can often provide you with inside information that can be invaluable in an interview. But let's say that you don't know anyone who works there—what can you do? Go to the source. Often, a receptionist can get you product catalogs, brochures, reports, or other literature that explains the purpose, products, or services of the organization. You can also find much of this information online at the company's Web site. If you study this information well, you will have more knowledge of the organization than most other applicants.

You can also go to the library and ask the librarian to help you locate any local or national information about the organization. You can often look up recent newspaper articles and, particularly for larger organizations, information in various industrial and other directories.

The more you know about the job, the industry, and the employer, the more likely you are to present yourself well in the interview. More importantly, you will be better able to evaluate whether a particular job is right for you.

Researching the Company

When doing research on a company, you want to focus on company missions, ethics, areas of recent growth, and weak spots. According to librarian Mary-Ellen Mort in Oakland, California, the best sources for information on local organizations are local newspaper articles, local directories, and area trade journals. Some libraries have clipping files of articles on area companies, CEOs, and industries. Ask a reference librarian for ranked lists of local companies in your field. Depending on the library's size, you may even lay your hands on annual reports and various promotional literature, too. If the library doesn't carry copies of these materials, request them from the organization itself.

If the organization is a small, privately owned company, this type of information may not be available at all. In that case, explore comparable companies and apply what you find. Don't forget—it's never a mistake to pick up the phone and talk with the organization's suppliers, customers, and current employees.

Online Resources for Company Research

This section provides some general sites for researching employers online (from *Best Career and Education Web Sites* by Rachel Singer Gordon and Anne Wolfinger). Remember that one of the best sources of information on a company can be its own Web site. Search for employer Web sites by using your favorite search engines.

> **Tip:** *Offer to drop by and pick up the organization's material in person rather than have it mailed to you. This action fosters several positives. It allows you to meet with the receptionist and make a positive impression with an insider (good news travels fast, especially when it concerns a future employee). It also strengthens an impression that you are well-organized and very interested. Finally, it forces you to travel the route in advance of an interview and scout out potentially slowing traffic patterns, confusing addresses, and so on.*

- **CorporateInformation.com (www.corporateinformation.com):** You have to register to use this company research site, but basic registration is free. Type a company's name into the search box on the front page to find information on specific companies, which includes a brief analysis from this site as well as links to articles and company profiles from other Web sites. Although much information is targeted to investors, you'll find useful background material for your job hunt as well. You can also pick a state to find information on every company the site covers in that state or use an alphabetical list to browse corporations. This site is best for information on large companies.

- **Google News (news.google.com):** Search and browse 4,000 news sources from leading search engine Google. Find the most up-to-date news stories on specific companies, or simply pick the Business section to read current articles. This site is a great way to keep current on industries and specific companies. You can find out what's going on before applying or in preparation for an interview. Articles stay in the index for 30 days.

- **SuperPages (www.superpages.com):** Verizon's SuperPages is an electronic Yellow Pages with a twist. Search for U.S. businesses by name and location, or browse by category. Each listing contains contact information as well as a Web site link when available, plus a map and driving directions. Register to create your own directory of saved listings. You can also search for businesses by geographic location if you're looking for potential places to apply in your area.

- **Thomas Register (www.thomasregister.com):** Thomas Register takes its print manuals online, allowing registered users to search for manufacturers and companies and view their catalogs and Web sites. Check out the demo to see how searching works and what information is included in manufacturer listings. Although the site is meant largely for locating suppliers, it's a useful way for job seekers to locate companies in their industry as well.

Company Research Tutorials

For tips and instructions on researching employers, check out these Web sites:

- **Industry Research Desk (www.virtualpet.com/industry/):** This 19-step process walks you through researching a specific company or a specific industry. A ton of links to useful resources are included among the steps, so take some time to explore. You'll also find ideas on potentially useful print resources that you can look through at your local public or college library.

- **Researching Companies Online (www.learnwebskills.com/company/):** This step-by-step tutorial from Internet trainer Debbie Flanagan contains surefire tips for locating free company and industry information on the Web. Topics here include locating company home pages, monitoring company news, learning about an industry, identifying international business resources, and researching nonprofit organizations. Each topic includes useful links and instructions, and you can also access her Web Search Strategies tutorial from here.

- **Riley Guide: Using the Internet to Do Job Search Research (www.rileyguide.com/jsresearch.html):** The first section provides general tips on doing effective Internet research, and the second gives specific advice on finding company information. This step-by-step tutorial shows you how to do research on all aspects of your job search, and it links to a number of sites for additional information and ideas.

Essential Questions Your Research Must Answer

Now that you've gathered all this raw data, how do you apply it to the interview? Here are some questions your research should answer:

- What is the prospective employer and what does it do?

- What has the organization done in the last three years?

- Where is the organization headed? What new products or services are on the horizon?

- What/who is the competition? Where is this organization at an advantage or disadvantage?

- What are the success factors?

- How can the job you are pursuing contribute to the organization's success?

Granted, translating columns of numbers and sales slogans into tangible answers to these questions takes some thoughtful application on your part. However, don't let it scare you into not even trying. For starters, pick up a copy of Lelia K. Kight's *Getting the Lowdown on Employers and a Leg Up on the Job Market* (Ten Speed Press) for some down-to-earth, instructive steps in interpreting annual reports. Be sure to read the CEO's message at the beginning of each report. This carefully crafted editorial sets the tone for the year past and the organization's direction in the years ahead.

Researching the Job

If you became aware of the job opening through an advertisement in a publication or online, start with the job posting that led you to it. Study it well and become aware of the skills, keywords, buzzwords, and concepts it uses. If any are unfamiliar to you, do your research and find out what they mean.

If you found out about the job through networking and don't have a job posting to refer to, you can request a description of the job from the company. Many companies are required to write detailed descriptions of the job's parameters and needed skills. This information is gold when you're preparing for an interview.

You can also use your network to find someone who works in a similar job. Ask that person what it takes to succeed in the job; then find ways to communicate these qualities to your interviewer.

Researching the Interviewer

Ultimately, when it comes to finding out information about your specific interviewer, you may have to rely on the telephone once again. If you know any of the current employees, politely and unobtrusively ask them about this person's style of work, how he or she spends the day, what types of behaviors earn a frown from this person, and so forth. The information you can dig up could be invaluable.

You'd be surprised what you can find out about people if you "Google" them on the Internet. Basically, go to your favorite search engine (such as Google or Yahoo!) and type the person's name, surrounded by quotation marks, in the search box. Several articles might come up, some of which could be about the person you will be speaking with. For instance, you might learn that your interviewer volunteered to train runners for the local charity marathon. Or you might hit pay dirt and find a press release about the company's new product that specifically quotes your interviewer. You have to use your judgment here, though, because lots of people in the world share the same name, and the information you dig up could be about an entirely different person.

Key Points: Chapter 3

- Being well-informed about the industry you want to join will help you present yourself well in the interview and during salary negotiations.

- Learning more about your career area can help you discover career paths you may not have considered before and better target your interview responses and resume to the skills your career requires.

- You can find information about the employer and the position you are applying for from former or current employees, trade publications, or the company's Web site or publications. This information is indispensable in preparing for an interview.

Chapter 4

Answering Key Interview Questions

Improving your performance in the interview even slightly can result in your getting a job offer over someone else. Many employers I've spoken with say that they would have hired someone if that person had just done a bit better in the interview. Spending a little time to learn how to answer the questions covered in this chapter can make an enormous difference to you in getting a job over other qualified applicants.

The 10 Most Frequently Asked Interview Questions—and How to Answer Them

In this section, I use the Three-Step Process from chapter 1 to create answers to the 10 questions you are most likely to be asked in an interview. For each question, I provide an analysis of what the question is really asking, followed by a strategy for answering it. I also provide one or more sample responses. These responses demonstrate the basic techniques, which you can then apply to your own interview situation.

Question #1: "Why Don't You Tell Me About Yourself?"

This is the classic open-ended interview question. You could start telling your life's history in two hours or less, but that is not what the interviewer wants to hear. Instead, such a question is a test of your ability to select what is important and communicate it clearly and quickly. Obviously, the interviewer expects you to relate your background to the position being considered.

There are two basic approaches to answering this question. One is to provide a brief response to the question as it is asked, and the other is to request a clarification of the question before answering it. In both cases, you would answer the question and then quickly turn your response to focus on the skills, experience, and training that prepared you for the sort of job you now want (see chapter 2 for more on discovering these). In other words, you want to relate what you say about yourself to the job at hand. Talk about your experiences as they relate to the position.

Sample Answer #1

If you answered the question as it was asked, you might say something like this:

> "I grew up in the Southwest and have one brother and one sister. My parents both worked and I was active in sports growing up. I always did well in school, and by the time I graduated from high school I had taken a year's worth of business courses. I knew then that I wanted to work in a business setting and had several part-time office jobs while still in high school. After high school I worked in a variety of business settings and learned a great deal about how various businesses run. For example, I was given complete responsibility for the daily operations of a wholesale distribution company that grossed over two million dollars a year. That was only three years after I graduated from high school. There I learned to supervise other people and solve problems under pressure. I also became more interested in the financial end of running a business and decided, after three years and three promotions, to seek a position where I could have more involvement in key strategies and long-term management decisions."

Notice how this applicant provided a few bits of positive personal history and then quickly turned the interviewer's attention to skills and experiences that directly related to the job this applicant was seeking.

Sample Answer #2

You could ask interviewers to help you focus on the information they really want to know with a response such as this:

> "There's so much to tell! Would you like me to emphasize my personal history, the special training and education I have that prepared me for this sort of position, or the skills and job-related experiences I have to support my objective?"

If you do this well, most employers will tell you what sorts of things they are most interested in, and you can then concentrate on giving them what they want.

Honesty is always the best policy, but that old adage doesn't rule out marketing yourself in the best light during an interview. Virtually all career counselors encourage job seekers to be positive about themselves and don't consider this positive spin as unethical in any way. But they also caution you to avoid taking credit for something you don't deserve, claiming to have experience you don't have, or bragging about your performance. You can talk up your achievements, awards, and promotions without misrepresenting yourself. A job interview is also not the place to talk about an unhappy childhood or make negative comments about past employers. Instead, focus on the positive by saying that your childhood helped you become self-motivated, resilient, and a hard worker.

Question #2: "Why Should I Hire You?"

Though this question is rarely asked this clearly, it is the question behind any other question that is asked. It has no hidden meaning.

Such a direct and fair question deserves a direct response. Why should employers hire you? The best response to this question provides advantages to employers, not to you. A good response gives proof that you can help them make more money by improving efficiency, reducing costs, increasing sales, or solving problems (by coming to work on time, improving customer service, organizing one or more operations, offering knowledge of a particular software or computer system, or bringing a variety of other talents to an organization).

Sample Answer

A person with considerable prior experience might offer this response:

> "You should hire me because I don't need to be trained and have a proven track record. I have more than 15 years of education and experience related to this position. More than six of those years have been in management positions similar to the one available here. In my last position, I was promoted three times in the six years I was there. I most recently had responsibility for supervising a staff of 15 and a warehousing operation that processed over 30 million dollars' worth of materials a year. In the last two years, I managed a 40 percent

increase in volume processed with only a 6 percent increase in expenses. I am hardworking and have earned a reputation as a dependable and creative problem solver. The opportunities here excite me. My substantial experience will help me to know how to approach the similar situations here. I am also willing to ask questions and accept advice from others. This willingness will be an important factor in taking advantage of what has already been accomplished here."

This job seeker's response emphasized the Prove-It Technique from chapter 1 and included a variety of specific numbers to support her accomplishments. Although she presented her skills and experience in a direct and confident way, she avoided a know-it-all attitude by being open to others' suggestions. She also made it clear that she wanted this particular job and why she should be considered for it.

Because having good reasons for why someone should hire you over others is so important to your job search success, I have included the brief activity that follows. Completing it will be a challenge unless you first complete some of the activities in chapter 2.

THE REASONS WHY SOMEONE SHOULD HIRE YOU

List the major advantages you offer an employer in hiring you over someone else. Emphasize your strengths. These could be personality traits, transferable skills, special training, prior experience, or anything else you think is important. These are the things to emphasize in your interview.

1. _____

   _____

   _____

2. _____

   _____

   _____

---

3. _____

_____

_____

Question #3: "What Are Your Major Strengths?"

Like the previous question, this one is quite direct and has little hidden meaning. This question allows you to focus on the credentials you have that are most important to doing well in the position you are seeking. Your response should emphasize your key adaptive or self-management skills. The decision to hire you is largely based on these skills; you can deal with the details of your specific job-related skills later. Remember that here, as elsewhere, your response must be brief and direct.

Sample Answer

This response is from a person who has little prior work experience related to the job he now seeks:

> "One of my major strengths is my ability to work hard toward a goal. Once I make a decision to accomplish something, it gets done and done well. For example, I graduated from high school four years ago. Many of my friends started working, and others went on to school. At the time I didn't know what I wanted to do, so furthering my education at that point did not make sense. The jobs I could get at the time didn't excite me either, so I looked into joining the Navy. I took the test and discovered a few things about myself that surprised me. For one thing, I was much better at understanding complex problems than my grades in high school would suggest. I signed up for a three-year hitch that included intensive training in electronics. I worked hard and graduated in the top 20 percent of my class. I was then assigned to monitor, diagnose, and repair an advanced electronics system that was worth about 20 million dollars. I was promoted several times to the

> position of Petty Officer and received an honorable discharge after my tour of duty. I now know what I want to do and am prepared to spend extra time learning whatever is needed to do well here."

Once you begin speaking about one of your strengths, the rest of your response often falls into place naturally, as this sample response illustrates. Remember to provide some proof of your skills, as this response did when citing results of Navy entrance testing and repeated advancement in a highly responsible position. These specifics about your skills can make a difference.

Question #4: "What Are Your Major Weaknesses?"

You must be prepared to answer this trick question. If you answer the question as it is asked, you could easily damage your chances of getting the job. By trying to throw you off guard, the employer can see how you might react in similar tough situations on the job. I have often asked this question to groups of job seekers, and I usually get one of two types of responses. The first response goes like this:

> "I really don't have any major weaknesses."

That response is untrue and evasive. The other type of response I usually get is an honest one like this:

> "Well, I am really disorganized. I suppose I should do better at that, but my life has just been too hectic, what with the bankruptcy and embezzlement charges and all."

Although this type of response might get an *A* for honesty, it gets an *F* for interview technique.

What's needed here is an honest, undamaging response followed by a brief, positive presentation to counter the negative. The best approach is to present a weakness in a way that does not harm—and could help—your ability to do a good job. Here are some examples:

Sample Answer #1

"Well, I have been accused by coworkers of being too involved in my work. I usually come in a little early to organize my day and stay late to get a project done on time."

Sample Answer #2

"I need to learn to be more patient. I often do things myself just because I know I can do them faster and better than someone else. This trait has not let me be as good at delegating tasks as I want to be. But I am working on it. I'm now spending more time showing others how to do the things I want done and that has helped. They often do better than I expect because I am clear about explaining what I want and how I want it done."

These responses could both be expanded with the Prove-It Technique, but they successfully use the Three-Step Process in answering a problem question, as outlined in chapter 1. In both cases, the answers responded to the question as it was asked, but they did so in a way that presented the weakness as a positive.

Question #5: "What Sort of Pay Do You Expect to Receive?"

If you are unprepared for this question, any response you give is likely to damage your ability to get a job offer. The employer wants you to name a number that can be compared to a figure the company has in mind. Suppose that the employer is looking to pay someone $36,000 a year. If you say you were hoping for $40,000, you will probably be eliminated from consideration. The employer will be afraid that, if you took the job, you may not stay. If you say you would take $29,000, you will make it nearly impossible to negotiate for a higher salary if you are offered the job. Or the employer might decide that your skills are worth less than what the job requires.

This question is designed to help the employer either eliminate you from consideration or save money at your expense. You could get lucky and name the salary the employer had in mind, but the stakes are too high for me to recommend that approach.

Employers often use discussions of pay in an initial interview to screen people out. Because you aren't likely to get a firm job offer in a first interview, your objective should be to create a positive impression and not be rejected. If the topic of pay does come up, avoid getting nailed down. Here are some things you could say:

> "Are you making me a job offer?" (A bit corny, yes, but you just might be surprised at the result.)

> "What salary range do you pay for positions with similar requirements?"

> "I'm very interested in the position, and my salary would be negotiable."

> "Tell me what you have in mind for the salary range."

> "I prefer to hear more about the position before I can come up with a solid number."

Put off discussion of pay until you are sure it's the real thing and not just part of a screening process. See chapter 8 for more information on how to talk money when the time is right.

Question #6: "How Does Your Previous Experience Relate to the Jobs We Have Here?"

This is another direct question that requires a direct response. If you have created a good impression up to this point, your response to this question is especially important. It requires you to overcome any weaknesses your background might present when you are compared to other job seekers. Here are some typical stumbling blocks:

- You are just out of school and have limited experience in this career.

- This is your first job, or you have not worked for a period of time.

- Your prior work experience is not a match for the tasks required in this job.

- Your previous level of responsibility was lower or higher than this job requires.

- You have had several jobs, but no clear career direction.

- You do not have the education or other credentials many other applicants might have.

Lead with your strengths. If it is obvious that other job seekers might have more education, more years of experience, or whatever qualifications you lack, acknowledge that, and then present your strengths. Use the standard Three-Step Process from chapter 1 to answer a problem question.

Sample Answer #1

"As you know, I have just completed an intensive program in the area of information technology. In addition, I have more than three years of work experience in a variety of business settings. That work experience included managing a small business during the absence of the owner. I learned to handle money there and do a variety of basic accounting tasks. I also inventoried and organized products worth over six hundred thousand dollars. These experiences helped me understand the importance of good information technology systems in a business setting. Although I am a recent information technology graduate, my previous business experience allows me to understand how to use what I have learned in practical and effective ways. My educational experience was very thorough, and I have more than 300 hours of interactive computer time as part of my course work. Because I am new to this career, I plan to work harder and will spend extra time as needed to meet any deadlines."

This response emphasizes transferable skills (knowledge of accounting procedures) and adaptive skills (meeting deadlines and working hard). This emphasis is necessary to counter a lack of previous work experience in the information technology area. In this situation, what was learned in school is also very important and should be emphasized as the equivalent of "real" work.

Sample Answer #2

"In my previous position, I used many of the same skills that are needed to do this job well. Even though it was in a different industry, managing a business requires the types of organizational and supervisory skills that I possess. Over the past seven years, I guided my region to become one of the most profitable in our company. Sales expanded an average of 30 percent per year during the years I worked there, and profits rose at a similar rate. Because this was a mature company, such performance was highly unusual. I received two promotions during those seven years and rose to the management level quickly. I was later told that no one had previously achieved this kind of advancement. I am now seeking a challenge in a smaller, growth-oriented company such as yours. I feel my experience and contacts have prepared me for this step in my career."

This response acknowledges that the previous career field differed from the one now being considered but emphasizes prior achievements and success. Accomplishing this level of success requires the use of all sorts of skills. The response also includes the motivation to move on to the challenge of a smaller organization.

Question #7: "What Are Your Plans for the Future?"

This question explores your motives for working. It asks whether you can be depended on to stay on at this job and work hard at it.

As always, your best approach is an honest one. I'm not encouraging you to reveal negative information, but you should be prepared to answer the employer's concern in a direct and positive way. Which issues are of concern to an employer depend on the details of your background.

For example:

- Will you be happy with the salary? (If not, might you leave?)
- Will you want to have a family? (If so, will you quit or cut your hours to raise children?)
- Do you have a history of leaving jobs after a short period of time? (If so, why won't you leave this one too?)

- Have you just moved to the area or do you appear to be a temporary or transient resident? (If so, you probably won't stay here long either, right?)

- Are you overqualified? (If so, what will keep you from going to a better job as soon as you find one?)

- Do you have the energy and commitment to advance in this job? (If not, who needs someone without energy and drive?)

- Might you appear to have some other reason to eventually become dissatisfied? (If so, the employer will certainly try to figure out what it is.)

Any of these factors, and others, can be of concern to an employer. If your situation presents an obvious problem, use the standard Three-Step Process for answering problem interview questions from chapter 1. If you feel you do not have any problem to defend, use steps #2 and #3 of the Three-Step Process to assure the employer that this is precisely the organization you want to stay with, grow with, and do well with for many years to come.

Sample Answer #1

This response is from a younger person or one just entering a new career:

> "I realize I need to establish myself in this field and am eager to get started. I've thought about what I want to do and am very sure my skills are the right ones to do well in this career. For example, I am good at dealing with people. In one position, I provided services to over 1,000 different people a week. During the 18 months I was there, I served well over 72,000 customers and not once did I get a formal complaint. In fact, I was often complimented on the attention I gave them. There I learned that I enjoy public contact and am delighted at the idea of taking on this position for that reason. I want to learn more about the business and grow with it. As my contributions and value to the organization increase, I hope to be considered for more responsible positions."

The employer wants to know that you will stay on the job and work hard for your pay. This response addresses that concern and helps the employer feel more comfortable. (Note that this response could be based on work experiences gained in a fast-food job!)

Sample Answer #2

This response is for a person with gaps in work history or various short-term jobs:

> "I've had a number of jobs (or one, or have been unemployed), and I have learned to value a good, stable position. The variety of my experiences is an asset because I have learned so many things I can now apply to this position. I am looking for a position where I can settle in, work hard, and stay put."

This response would be acceptable, but a better one would be a bit longer and include some proof of the job seeker's skills. The ideal place to introduce a story would have been right before the last sentence. Some positions, such as sales-oriented ones, require you to be ambitious and perhaps even a bit aggressive. Other jobs have requirements particular to the career field or specific organization. You can't always predict exactly what an employer might want, but you should have a good idea based on what skills that job requires. A good answer to this question tells the employer that you have what the position requires. You simply need to say so.

Question #8: "What Will Your Former Employers (or Teachers, References, Warden...) Say About You?"

The employer wants to know about your adaptive skills. Are you easy to get along with? Are you a good worker? Your former employers and other references may tell of any problems you had—or they may not. As you know, many employers check your references before they hire you, so if anything you say as a response to this question does not match what a former employer or other reference says, it could be bad news for you.

Be certain to discuss your job search plans with former employers. Do the same with anyone else who may be contacted for a reference. Clearly tell them the type of job you now seek and why you are prepared to do well in it. If a previous employer may say something negative, discuss this issue openly with that employer and find out what he or she will say in advance.

If you were fired or resigned under pressure, you can often negotiate what would be said to a prospective employer. Lots of successful people have had personality conflicts with previous employers. If these conflicts are presented openly and in the best light possible, many interviewers are likely to understand. It may also be wise to get a written letter of reference, particularly from a not-too-enthusiastic former employer. Such an employer is rarely brave enough to write you a totally negative letter. The letter may be enough to satisfy a potential employer. Larger organizations often don't allow employees to give references; if you are worried about a negative reference, this rule may be a great relief to you. Check it out by calling your former employers and finding out their policy.

If possible, use references that will say nice things about you. If your ex-boss won't, find someone who will. Often, an interviewer appreciates an honest response. If you failed in a job, telling the truth is often the best policy. Tell it like it was, but *do not* be too critical of your old boss. If you do, it will make you sound like a person who blames others and does not accept responsibility. If you were partly at fault, admit it, but quickly take the opportunity to say what you learned from the experience.

Sample Answer

"My three former employers will all say I work hard, am very reliable, and am loyal. The reason I left my previous job, however, is the result of what I can only call a personality conflict. I was deeply upset by this but decided that it was time I parted with my former employer. You can call and get a positive reference, but I thought it only fair to tell you. I still respect my ex-boss and am grateful for the experience I gained at that job. While there, I received several promotions, and as my authority increased, there were more conflicts. Our styles were just not the same. I had no idea the problem was so serious because I was so involved in my work. That was my error, and I have since learned to pay more attention to interpersonal matters."

This response could be strengthened by the introduction of positive skills along with an example that includes some proof to support them.

Question #9: "Why Are You Looking for This Sort of Position and Why Here?"

The employer wants to know if you are the sort of person who is looking for any job, anywhere. If you are, she or he will not be impressed.

Employers look for people who want to do what needs to be done. They rightly assume that such a person will work harder and be more productive than one who simply sees it as "just a job." People who have a good reason to seek a particular sort of position are seen as more committed and more likely to stay on the job longer. The same is true for people who want to work in a particular organization. A good thing about this question is that it allows you to present your skills and other credentials for wanting this particular job.

Knowing in advance which jobs are a good match for your skills and interests is most important. In responding to this question, mention your motivations for selecting this career objective, the special skills you have that the position requires, and any special training or credentials you have which relate to the position.

The question has two parts. The first is "Why this position?" The second is "Why here?" If you have a reason for selecting the type of organization you are considering or have even selected this particular organization as highly desirable, be prepared to explain why. Use the research techniques in chapter 3 to become as informed as possible.

Sample Answer

An experienced manager or a sharp office worker could use this type of response:

> "I've spent a lot of time considering various careers, and I think that this is the best area for me. The reason is that this career requires many of my strongest skills. For example, my abilities in analyzing and solving problems are two of the skills I enjoy using most. In a previous position, I would often become aware of a problem no one had noticed and develop a solution. In one situation, I suggested a plan that resulted in reducing customer returns of leased equipment by 15 percent. That may not sound like much, but the result was an increase in retained leases of more than $250,000 a year. The plan cost about $100 to implement. This particular organization seems to be the type that would let me use similar problem-solving skills. It is well-run, growing rapidly, and open to new ideas. Your sales went up 30 percent last year, and you are getting ready to introduce several major new products. If I work hard

and prove my value here, I feel I would have the opportunity to stay with the business as it grows—and grow with it."

This response uses the Prove-It Technique nicely.

Question #10: "Why Don't You Tell Me About Your Personal Situation?"

A good interviewer will rarely ask this question so directly. If this question is asked this directly, simply ask the person something like, "What is it you would like to know?" In this way you show them that you have nothing to hide. More often, interviewers use casual and friendly conversation to get the information they want. In most cases, the interviewer is digging for information that would indicate you are unstable or undependable.

Other issues may be of concern to an employer as well. Often, these are based on assumptions the person has about people with certain characteristics. These beliefs are often irrelevant (and some may seem to be in bad taste or even illegal), but if the employer wonders whether you can be depended upon, dealing with these doubts is in your own best interest. Be aware that even your casual conversation should always avoid reference to a potential problem area. In responding to a question about your personal situation, be friendly and positive. Your objective is to give employers the answer that they need to have, not just the one they may seem to ask. See chapter 5 for guidelines on handling illegal questions.

Examples of Appropriate Answers

The following responses address the personal issues that employers are most concerned about.

Young children at home:

> "I have two children, both in school. Child care is no problem because they stay with a good friend."

Single head of household:

> "I'm not married and have two children at home. It is very important to me to have a steady income, so child care is no problem."

Young and single:

> "I'm not married, and if I should marry, that would not change my plans for a full-time career. For now, I can devote my full attention to my career."

Just moved here:

> "I've decided to settle here in Depression Gulch permanently. I've rented an apartment, and the six moving vans are unloading there now."

Relatives, upbringing:

> "I am one of three children. Both of my parents still live within an hour's flight from here, and I see them several times a year."

Leisure time:

> "My time is family-centered when I'm not working. I'm also active in several community organizations and spend at least some time each week in church activities."

All of these responses could be expanded on, but they should give you an idea of the types of approaches you can take with your own answers. The message you want to give is that your personal situation will not hurt your ability to work and, indeed, could help it. If your personal life does disrupt your work, expect most employers to lose patience quickly. It is not their problem, nor should it be.

94 Other Frequently Asked Interview Questions

The following list presents questions most often asked by recruiters who interview new graduates at college campuses. Although some of the questions may not apply to your situation, they give you a good idea of the types of questions a trained interviewer might ask you in an interview. Look over the list and check any that would be hard for you to answer well. Then practice coming up with positive answers for those problem questions using the Three-Step Process for answering interview questions that has been used in this chapter.

1. What are your future vocational plans?

2. In what school activities have you participated? Why? Which did you enjoy the most?

3. How do you spend your spare time? What are your hobbies?

4. What type of position most interests you?

5. Why do you think you might like to work for our company?

6. What jobs have you held? How were they obtained?

7. What courses did you like best? Least? Why?

8. Why did you choose your particular field of work?

9. What percentage of your school expenses did you earn? How?

10. How did you spend your vacations while in school?

11. What do you know about our company?

12. Do you feel that you have received a good general training?

13. What qualifications do you have that make you feel that you will be successful in your field?

14. What extracurricular offices have you held?

15. What are your ideas on salary?

16. How do you feel about your family?

17. How interested are you in sports?

18. If you were starting school all over again, what would you do differently?

19. Can you forget your education and start from scratch?

20. Do you prefer any specific geographic location? Why?

21. Do you have a girlfriend/boyfriend? Is it serious?

22. How much money do you hope to earn at age _____?

23. Why did you decide to go to the school you attended?

24. How did you rank in your graduating class in high school? Other schools?

25. Do you think that your extracurricular activities were worth the time you devoted to them? Why?

26. What do you think determines a person's progress in a good company?

27. What personal characteristics are necessary for success in your chosen field?

28. Why do you think you would like this particular type of job?

29. What is your father's occupation?

30. Tell me about your home life during the time you were growing up.

31. Are you looking for a permanent or temporary job?

32. Do you prefer working with others or by yourself?

33. What types of people are your best friends?

34. What kind of boss do you prefer?

35. Are you primarily interested in making money?

36. Can you take instructions without feeling upset?

37. Tell me a story.

38. Do you live with your parents? Which of your parents has had the most profound influence on you?

39. How did previous employers treat you?

40. What have you learned from some of the jobs you have held?

41. Can you get recommendations from previous employers?

42. What interests you about our product or service?

43. What was your record in military service?

44. Have you ever changed your major field of interest? Why?

45. When did you choose a major?

46. How did your grades after military service compare with those you previously earned?

47. Do you feel you have done the best work of which you are capable?

48. How did you happen to go to postsecondary school?

49. What do you know about opportunities in the field in which you are trained?

50. How long do you expect to work?

51. Have you ever had any difficulty getting along with fellow students and faculty? Fellow workers?

52. Which of your school years was most difficult?

53. What is the source of your spending money?

54. Do you own any life insurance?

55. Have you saved any money?

56. Do you have any debts?

57. How old were you when you became self-supporting?

58. Do you attend church?

59. Did you enjoy school?

60. Do you like routine work?

61. Do you like regular work?

62. What size city do you prefer?

63. When did you first contribute to family income?

64. What is your major weakness?

65. Define cooperation.

66. Will you fight to get ahead?

67. Do you demand attention?

68. Do you have an analytical mind?

69. Are you eager to please?

70. What do you do to keep in good physical condition?

71. How do you usually spend Sunday?

72. Have you had any serious illness or injury?

73. Are you willing to go where the company sends you?

74. What job in our company would you choose if you were entirely free to do so?

75. Is it an effort for you to be tolerant of persons with a background and interests different from your own?

76. What types of books have you read?

77. Have you plans for further education?

78. What types of people seem to rub you the wrong way?

79. Do you enjoy sports as a participant? As an observer?

80. Have you ever tutored another student?

81. What jobs have you enjoyed the most? The least? Why?

82. What are your own special abilities?

83. What job in our company do you want to work toward?

84. Would you prefer a large or a small company? Why?

85. What is your idea of how industry operates today?

86. Do you like to travel?

87. How about overtime work?

88. What kind of work interests you?

89. What are the disadvantages of your chosen field?

90. Do you think that grades should be considered by employers? Why or why not?

91. Are you interested in research?

92. If married, how often do you entertain at home?

93. To what extent do you use liquor?

94. What have you done that shows initiative and willingness to work?

Key Points: Chapter 4

- Prepare yourself for an interview by thinking through your answers to the most common interview questions.

- Answer difficult questions honestly, but always present yourself in a positive light.

- Use your responses to the interview questions to emphasize how your skills fit the employer's needs and reassure the interviewer that you are the best choice for this position.

Chapter 5

Handling Tough Interview Questions and Unusual Situations

The odds are very high that you could be eliminated from consideration for jobs based on your answer (or, more likely, your lack of a good answer) to one or more of the interview questions or issues I bring up in this chapter. None of us is perfect. We all have things about ourselves and our past that could be or will be a problem for some employers. You may have "too much" or "too little" education or training or gaps in your work history; you may be "too old" or "too young" or have other characteristics that concern some employers. Some of these things you can't change, but it is your responsibility to make these matters less of an issue in a decision to hire you over someone else.

I mentioned earlier in this book that about 80 percent of all people who get interviews do not, according to employer surveys, do a good job in answering one or more interview questions. These problem questions vary for each person and depend on your situation. The job seeker's inability to answer these problem questions is a very big obstacle in the job search and has kept many good people from getting jobs they are perfectly capable of handling. They didn't get those jobs because they failed to convince employers that they had the skills and other characteristics to do the job. In many cases they left employers with a sense that there was an unresolved problem. That is to say that the job seekers would have gotten the job offer if they had done better in the interview.

One of the difficulties with problem questions is that the employer often does not ask these questions in a clear way, or does not ask them at all. For example, if you live a long distance from the employer's job site, the interviewer may be wondering why you would be willing to commute daily to a distant location. His concern may be that you would leave once you found a job closer to home. The interviewer may never directly ask you about working so far away from home, so you would not have the opportunity to address his concern, and that job is likely to go to someone else. It is not fair, but that is the way it is.

So the issue here is not your ability to *do* the job, rather the issue is your ability to communicate clearly that you *can and will* do the job well. This chapter helps you quickly identify problem questions an employer may pose about your particular situation and gives you some ways to handle them in a truthful and positive way.

Dealing with Illegal Questions

Technically, this is a free country. Our Constitution gives all of us the right of free speech, including the right of an employer to ask inappropriate questions. (Some people would disagree, however, saying that an employer does not have this right.) Employers can ask almost anything they want in an interview or on an application. They can ask offensive questions, personal questions, and even just plain dumb questions.

The problem arises when employers use that information to hire one person over another based on certain criteria, such as race, gender, or religion. That action is illegal, although it is very difficult to prove that an employer actually does that. The truth is that some employers base their hiring decisions on things that should not be an issue at all—things such as age, religious affiliation, weight, family status, physical beauty, race or ethnic background, and other inappropriate criteria.

As a job seeker, the more important issue might be whether or not you want the job. If you want to insist that you do not have to answer a certain question, fine. However, realize that the question was probably intended to find out whether you will be a good employee. That *is* a legitimate concern for an employer, and you have the responsibility, if you want the job, of letting the employer know you will be a good choice.

There are situations (thankfully, very rare) where an interviewer's questions are offensive. They may be offensive in the way they are asked or because of the type of questions they are. If that is the case, you could fairly conclude that you would not consider working for such a person. You just might, in this sort of situation, tell that employer what you think of him or her. You might also consider reporting that employer to the authorities. (A follow-up thank-you note for the interview would not be required in this case.)

Know the Laws That Protect You from Discrimination

Two major laws come into play in cases of hiring discrimination:

- Title VII of the Civil Rights Act, which was enacted in 1964 and is still very much in effect, makes discrimination on the basis of race, gender, religion, or national origin illegal in hiring discussions.

- The Americans with Disabilities Act, which passed in 1990 and was put into effect in 1992, requires that an employer provide an equal opportunity for an individual with a disability to participate in the job application process and to be considered for a job.

A specific job might require an answer to some questions that might appear to be illegal for other jobs. For example, firefighters need to be in good physical condition because they may be required to climb a ladder carrying 100 or more pounds. Therefore strength and health-related questions are acceptable in interviews for firefighters. Bartenders need to be at least 21 years old, so the interviewer can ask about age when interviewing a bartender. These are examples of legitimate job-related questions that an employer can ask when interviewing people for these jobs. In general, an employer is not allowed to ask for or consider information that is not related to a person's ability to do the job.

> **Tip:** *If you think that you have been discriminated against in the job hiring process, visit the U.S. Equal Employment Opportunity Commission Web site at www.eeoc.gov. This Web site contains guidelines for determining whether discrimination has occurred and instructions for filing a complaint.*

Turn Your Negative into a Positive

So let's assume that you are concerned that you might be unfairly discriminated against and you are reasonably well-qualified for the job you seek. First, understand that highly qualified people with no apparent problems often are unable to obtain jobs after many interviews. The labor market can be very competitive, and others may get the jobs simply because they have better qualifications. In addition, less-qualified people often get offers simply because they do well in the interview. Because you can't easily change your personal situation, you need to improve your interview skills to give you an edge.

Begin by considering how an employer might be legitimately concerned about you or your situation. Might the employer think that you would be less reliable, less productive, or in some other way less capable of doing the job? If so (and the typical answer here is that some might), practice an answer that indicates the problem will not be an issue in your case.

For example, if you have young children at home (an issue, by the way, that men are rarely asked about), it is to your advantage to mention that you have excellent child care and don't expect any problems. In addition, look for a way to present your "problem" as an advantage. Perhaps you could say that your additional responsibilities make it even more important for you to be well-organized, a skill that you have developed over many years and fully expect to apply in the new job. In other words, turn your disadvantage into an advantage.

Answer Open-Ended Questions Effectively

Employers want to get the information they need to make a safe, profitable hiring decision. You, the candidate, want some privacy and a fair chance to be considered based on your merits. Open-ended interview questions generally achieve both goals.

For instance, instead of an employer asking "Are you living with anyone?" she may phrase the question as "Do you foresee any situations that would prevent you from traveling or relocating?" The employer may want to know whether you have any limitations regarding work schedule or whether you have roots in the area that will encourage you to stay. The less direct question allows you to decide what information about your private life applies to the job at hand. Of course, if you are not prepared for such a question, you could provide information that might damage your chances for getting the job.

So, you see, employers often want to know details of your personal situation for legitimate reasons. They want to be sure that you can be depended on to stay on the job and work hard. Your task in the interview is to provide information indicating that, yes, you can be counted on to do the job. If you don't get that idea across, you will probably not be considered for the job.

Help with Specific Problem Interview Situations

This section deals with issues most people experience and that are often legitimate issues for an employer to explore. These issues include things such as gaps in your employment or being fired from a previous job. Employers are more likely to ask about these matters in a direct way.

Even the suggestion that some of the things in this chapter might be regarded as "problems" by an employer will make some people angry. For example, some would object to any mention that someone over 50 might experience discrimination in the labor market—although anyone over 50 knows that their age makes it harder to get a good job. Others resent that employers would even consider such things as race, religion, national origin, child care, and other "politically sensitive" matters in evaluating people for employment. But some employers do consider these things, despite the fact it is unfair or even illegal to do so.

Employers are simply people. They want to be assured that you will stay on the job for a reasonable length of time and do well. Sometimes, you just need to work harder to get this message across to them. You also have to realize that very few interviewers have had any formal interview training. They are merely trying to do their best and may, in the process, bumble a bit. They may ask questions that, technically, they should not. Consider forgiving them in advance for this, especially if their intent is simply to find out whether you are likely to be reliable. That is a legitimate concern on their part, and you will often have to help them find out that, in your case, their concerns are unwarranted.

In that context, I suggest you consider your situation in advance and be able to present to the employer that, in your case, being "overqualified," having children, being over 50, being a new graduate, or whatever your situation is simply not a problem at all and might even be an advantage.

Gaps in Your Work History

Some of the most accomplished people I know have been out of work at one time or another. About one out of five people in the workforce experiences some unemployment each year. Unemployment is not a sin, and most bosses have experienced it themselves, as have I.

The traditional resume technique is to write "20XX to Present" when referring to your most recent job, which makes it look as if you are still employed. If you use this trick, however, realize that it puts you in an uncomfortable position right away. One of the first things you will have to do in the interview is explain that this is not actually the case. Some employers will assume you are misrepresenting other facts about your situation as well—not a good impression for you to create.

Many people have gaps in their work history. If you have a legitimate reason for major gaps, such as going to school or having a child, tell the interviewer in a matter-of-fact way; don't apologize or act embarrassed about it. You could, however, add details about a related activity you did during that period that would strengthen your qualifications for the job at hand. This kind of detail reinforces that you aren't out of touch with what that employer needs; you merely chose not to actively practice it for a while.

During the conversation, it may help to refer to dates in years rather than months. This is accurate and avoids showing short job gaps. For example, if asked when you worked in the restaurant business, reply, "from 2003 to 2005" rather than "from November 2003 to June 2005." Of course, if pressed, give the exact dates without hesitation.

Being Fired

I remember looking for a new job after having been fired from my previous one. Actually, I was replaced as a result of internal politics. I hadn't done anything wrong other than to be associated with the wrong boss, one who had lost favor. Still, I feared that the people who remained behind would not give me good references. And it was awkward explaining to potential employers just why I wasn't still working there.

Lots of people get fired, and it often hurts their chances of getting some jobs. In some cases, employers are afraid that you will be a problem to them. Of course, if you were fired for just cause, you need to learn from the experience and change your behavior or consider another career. However, in most cases, job seekers harm their own chances of finding a new job more than being fired does.

Know How to Explain Your Situation

When you don't know how to explain your situation, you don't do a good job in interviews. Job seekers too often leave the potential employer wondering just what happened at the last job and, not knowing any different,

© JIST Works

assuming the worst. Leaving an employer with the thought that you are hiding something is a bad way to make a good impression. As a result, you don't get job offers.

Many employers tell me they will not hire someone unless they know why the person left his or her last job. They want to be sure that you are not a potential problem employee. You definitely will have to deal with this issue if you want to get hired. The good news here is that many employers have been fired themselves. Normally, people in charge alienate some people or have had interpersonal conflicts or other difficult situations—it goes along with being in charge. If you have a reasonable explanation, many inter-viewers will understand because they have had similar experiences.

So if you have lost a job, the best policy is usually to tell the truth. Avoid saying negative things about your last employer. Think about how you can put a positive spin on what happened. If you are not a big problem to work with, say so—and explain how you are very good at the things that *this* job requires. Tell the truth of what happened in your past job in an objective way and quickly turn to presenting the skills you have to do the job under discussion.

Negotiate for Better References

Another very important thing to do if you have been fired is to make sure that you negotiate with your previous employer about what he or she will say when giving you a reference. Ask for a written letter of reference, too. You can often negotiate this so that you won't be harmed as much as you might fear. These negotiations can help offset a negative past employer who just may have a simple personality conflict with you. This kind of conflict happens a lot, and it doesn't have to hurt you as much as you may think. Because almost everyone will lose his or her job once, you are in good company.

Get an alternative reference. Although you might have had a conflict with a previous boss, there are often others at your previous place of employ-ment who thought well of you. If so, you should try to get written recom-mendations from them in advance. You should also contact those people to find out how they might help if asked to provide a reference.

Changing Careers or Job History Unrelated to Your Current Job Objective

Chances are this issue isn't as important as you may assume. Sure, the interviewer is curious and wants to get to know you better, but if your past experience were a real barrier, you wouldn't have been invited for an interview in the first place. Stick to a planned schedule of emphasizing your skills and how they relate to the job you are discussing. For instance, a teacher who wants to become a real estate sales agent could point to her hobby of investing in and fixing up old houses. She could cite superior communication skills and an ability to motivate students in the classroom.

Look up the job descriptions of your old jobs and the ones you want now, and find skills that are common to both. Then emphasize those skills in your interviews. The work you did in chapter 2 will also help you document the skills and other strengths you have to support your current job objective.

Recently Moved

Employers are often concerned that someone who has recently moved to an area does not have roots there and may soon leave. If you are new to the area, make sure the employer knows you are there to stay. Provide a simple statement that presents you as a stable member of the community rather than someone with a more transient lifestyle. It may be helpful to mention any family or friends who may live nearby or other reasons you plan to stay in the area.

Military Experience

Employers who have not had military experience themselves often have misconceptions about those with military experience. The truth is that military people are just like everyone else, except that they are perhaps just a bit more responsible than the average person. Some of the stereotypes of military people can work in your favor; some don't.

Here are some common problem areas and suggestions for dealing with these preconceptions in a positive way:

- **Employers want people who can get along with others.** Some people assume military personnel are overly aggressive. Not true, of course, but you can easily handle this stereotype by being friendly. If you think this may be an issue, emphasize community service you have done, the importance of family and friends to you, and things you have done in and outside of the military that helped others.

- **Employers need people who work well in teams and solve problems.** Another common misconception is that military personnel are too likely to follow orders rather than be creative. More and more jobs require the ability to work as part of a self-directed team that is expected to solve problems with creative input from each member. The truth is that the military has been training with team cooperation and creative problem solving for many years. To overcome any negative stereotypes, you simply need to emphasize your team-building and problem-solving skills and experiences.

- **Employers may wonder why you left or assume that you don't have "civilian" skills.** Most people don't realize how large the military is and that each year more than 300,000 people leave it. Be sure to bring up why you left the military to put the interviewer's mind at rest that it had nothing to do with the concept of being fired. In most cases, ex-military people have served their country well, have benefited from excellent and expensive training, are more educated and technologically trained than the average person their age, and have had far more management experience or other responsibility than the average job seeker. The fact is that ex-military are among the most talented and dedicated people available; they are people who have worked hard and have a proven track record for getting difficult things done. Your responsibility in the interview is to make sure the employer knows these things about you.

- **Use civilian dress and language.** To reinforce your abilities as a civilian worker, avoid wearing military tie pins, rings, or other military jewelry or indicators. Completely avoid using any military jargon and replace it with terms that civilians use. Emphasize job-related and other skills you have that are needed in the civilian jobs you seek. The Web site at www.careerOINK.com has crosswalks from military to civilian jobs. The descriptions list the skills needed in these jobs. Emphasize these skills and give examples of when you used them and any results you obtained. Do emphasize that your military experience developed qualities that are important to all employers, including discipline, responsibility, and dependability.

The Turtling Technique

Like a turtle on its back, a problem is a problem only if you leave it that way. By turning it over ("turtling" is what I have come to call this), you can often turn a perceived disadvantage into an advantage. Take a look at these examples to understand what I mean:

- **Too old:** "I am a very stable worker requiring very little training. I have been dependable all my life, and I am at a point in my career where I don't plan on changing jobs. I still have 10 years of working until I plan on retiring. How long has the average young person stayed here?"

- **Too young:** "I don't have any bad work habits to break, so I can be quickly trained to do things the way you want. I plan on working hard to get established. I'll also work for less money than a more experienced worker."

You can use the Turtling Technique on most problem questions to turn what some may see as a negative into, in your case, a positive.

Negative References

Most employers do not contact your previous employers unless you are being seriously considered as a candidate for the job. If you fear that one of your previous employers may not give you a positive reference, here are some things you can do:

- **List someone other than your former supervisor as a reference.** Tap someone who knew your work there and who will put in a good word for you.

- **Discuss the issue in advance with your previous employer and negotiate what he or she will say.** Even if it's not good, at least you know what they are likely to say and can prepare potential employers in advance.

- **Get a written letter of reference.** In many cases, employers will not give references over the phone or e-mail (or negative references at all) for fear of being sued. Presenting a letter of reference ensures that you know what is said about your performance.

Criminal Record

A resume or application should never include negative information. So if you have ever been in trouble with the law, you would certainly not mention it in these documents. Newer laws prohibit an employer from including such general questions on an application as "Have you ever been arrested?" and limit formal inquiries to "Have you ever been convicted of a felony?"

In this country, we are technically innocent until proven guilty, and that is why employers are no longer allowed to consider an arrest record in a hiring decision. Being arrested and being guilty are two different things. Arrests for minor offenses (misdemeanors) are also not supposed to be considered in a hiring decision. The argument has been that minorities and urban youth are more likely to have arrest records and consideration of arrest records in a hiring decision is, therefore, discriminatory.

A felony conviction is a different matter. These crimes are more serious, and current employment laws do allow an employer to ask for and get this information and to use it in making certain hiring decisions. For example, few employers would hire an accountant who had been convicted of stealing money from a previous employer. An employer also can consider certain types of arrest records in making certain hiring decisions. For example, few employers would place a person who has been arrested for or convicted of child molesting in charge of a day-care facility or youth program.

If you have an arrest or conviction record that an employer has a legal right to inquire about, my advice is to avoid looking for jobs where your record would be a negative. The accountant in the previous example should consider changing careers. Even if the accountant did get a job by concealing his or her criminal history, that person could be fired at any time in the future. Instead, I might suggest that person consider selling accounting software, starting his or her own business, or getting into a completely different career unrelated to managing money.

As always, your interview should emphasize what you can do rather than what you can't. If you choose your career direction wisely and present a convincing argument that you can do the job well, many employers will, ultimately, overlook previous mistakes. As you prove yourself and gain good work experience, your distant past becomes less and less important.

Background Checks, Polygraphs, or Other Tests?

Many employers screen applicants before hiring. Screening is more common for jobs where theft can be a problem, for jobs that involve work with children, and for positions that require driving. Background checks may include drug screening, credit history, criminal history, verification of education and training, checks with past employers, and other inquiries depending on the position. In some cases an employer will not consider hiring anyone who does not agree to these background checks. Some employers are also using computerized or paper tests to identify people who are likely to be dishonest or have other personality-driven job-related problems.

In general, you need to convince an employer that you can be trusted to do a good job. If you have done a good job in preparing your responses, I suggest that you agree to background checks for jobs that interest you. If you have a serious problem in your background, you need to consider in advance how you will handle employer requests to check your background.

If you do have a problem that is likely to prevent you from getting a job if an employer becomes aware of it, avoid careers and jobs where your past would be a problem. Use job search methods that are less likely to require this information as part of the screening process. You can then explain your situation and why it is not a problem after you get a job offer.

Sensitive Questions About Your Personal Situation or Status

Many people consider the issues in this section, such as age, race, and gender, inappropriate for an employer to consider when making a decision to hire. Employers are much more likely to use indirect questions regarding these concerns.

Most employers are wise enough to avoid making decisions based on things that should not matter. They will hire someone who convinces them that he or she can do the job well. A good interview allows you to discuss your strengths without lying about them. Your handling of the interview can assure the interviewer that you are not a stereotype. But in order to prevent misconceptions, you must know what these stereotypes might be and address them.

For this reason, even if your "problem" does not come up in the interview because the law forbids the question or the interviewer is too uncomfortable to ask, bringing it up and dealing with it is likely to be to your advantage, especially if you think that an employer might wonder about the issue or that it might hurt you if you don't address it. However you handle the interview, the ultimate question you have to answer is "Why should I hire you?" so provide a good answer, even if the question is not asked quite so directly (see chapter 4 for advice on answering this question well).

"Too Old"

Older workers—particularly those over 50—have a harder time finding new jobs in the labor market. This group of workers includes a lot of highly qualified managers, technicians, and professionals in trade, manufacturing, and other industries who have lost jobs due to layoffs, downsizing, and other reasons not related to performance. About a third of these displaced workers end up getting higher paying, better jobs; another third get jobs that pay about the same; and the last third end up much worse off.

Why do older workers have such difficulty finding new jobs? There are some commonsense reasons that few people seem to want to talk about. Many older workers have not kept up with the latest technologies, and their skills are no longer in demand. Younger workers often have better training and technical skills and win jobs over older workers without these skills. However, I think there are other reasons that have to do with money and employer assumptions about being "overqualified."

People with more experience tend to be paid more. As anyone who has been in the labor market recently knows, the competition for higher-paying jobs is often intense. Unemployment statistics indicate that the more you make, the longer your job search is likely to be. A rule of thumb is that it takes one month per $10,000 in annual pay to find a new job. If you make $50,000 a year, plan on it taking five months to find a replacement job at that level of income. Of course, this may fluctuate somewhat depending on unemployment rates and the general health of the economy, but it's a reasonable estimate of the average length of time it takes to find a job at various levels of income (though it could take much less, if you use more effective job search methods).

In hiring someone new, most employers try to avoid hiring someone who was paid more in his or her previous position. Why? Because they fear that the person earning less than he or she is used to will be unhappy and will leave as soon as a better-paying job is available. One of the reasons employers hire a person with less experience is that they figure that such a person will be more satisfied with the pay he or she gets. In addition, many of the new jobs being created in the last decade are in smaller companies that just can't pay as much as many more established firms.

However, in the face of this concern about money, there are some things you can do:

- **Realize that many of the growing small businesses are run by older workers who know what they are doing.** Experienced older workers have started businesses and consultancies in droves. If you're not ready to start your own business, put your experience to work by approaching businesses and telling how you can help them do even better.

- **Be specific.** If you know how to develop product, manage, sell, or make any significant contribution, go to the places that need your skills and tell the person in charge what you can do. If you can convince employers that you can help them make more money than you cost, they may just create a job for you. Make sure that you present your substantial experience and good work history as an advantage. For example, you can probably be immediately productive and are likely to be more reliable than a younger worker.

- **Don't give up.** Someone out there needs what you can do, but you will have to go out and find them.

Don't let negative preconceptions about age discourage you—there are plenty of ways to combat them effectively during the job interview. For starters, understand that there are fewer younger workers now, so employers have no option but to compete for the qualified older workers.

To push the interviewer along that path, present your wealth of experience and maturity as an advantage rather than a disadvantage. Older workers often have some things going for them that younger workers do not. Emphasize your loyalty to previous employers, and highlight accomplishments that occurred over a period of time. If you encounter hesitation after the first interview, meet the fear head-on with a question such as "Are you concerned about compensation?" or "If I could reduce your costs significantly, would you be willing to make me a job offer?"

If you have more than 15 years of work experience, draw upon your more recent work for examples of work habits and successes. Select recent activities that best support your ability to do the job you are now seeking and put the emphasis on them. You don't automatically have to provide many details on your work history from earlier times unless doing so is clearly to your advantage.

Overqualified/Too Much Experience

It doesn't seem to make sense that you could have too much experience, but some employers may think so. They may fear you will not be satisfied with the job that is available and that, after a while, you will leave for a better one. What an employer needs is some assurance of why this would not be the case for you. If you are looking for a job with higher pay and you communicate this in some way during the interview, it is quite likely that the employer will not offer you a job for fear that you will soon leave.

After a period of unemployment, most people become more willing to set-tle for less than they had hoped for. If you are willing to accept jobs where you may be defined as overqualified, consider not presenting some of your educational or work-related credentials on your resume or at interviews—although I do not necessarily recommend doing this. Be prepared to explain in the interview why you *do* want this particular job and how your wealth of experience is a positive and not a negative.

Go out of your way to assure the interviewer that you aren't a job hopper. Maintain high enthusiasm for the organization's future, and present ways you could grow in this position. Suggest how you could assist other depart-ments, solve long-term problems, build profit, and use your experience to help out in other ways.

"Too Young"

Younger people need to present their youth as an asset rather than a liability. For example, perhaps you are willing to work for less money, accept less desirable tasks, work longer or less convenient hours, or do other things that a more experienced worker might not want to do. If this is true, you should say so in the interview. Emphasize the time and dedication you put into school projects. Above all, conduct yourself with maturity and show some genuine enthusiasm and energy.

If you are turned down in favor of a more experienced worker, don't despair. Keep ham-mering away at your particular skills, your trainability, and your available years of dedi-cation. Keep doing this, and some employer will be happy to hire you.

> **Tip:** *Remember that interviewers are also calculating salary requirements during the interview. They don't want to waste their time interviewing someone who will not accept their offer, even though they may have some flexibility to offer more for the right per-son. Your task is to not discuss money until the offer is made. See chapter 8 for tips on negotiating pay.*

New Graduate/Not Enough Experience

Every spring, newspapers across the country blast headlines about how difficult it is for today's graduates to find jobs in their areas of study. Before you start believing the bad press too much, keep in mind that such articles show only one side of the story. Yes, many new grads do find it difficult to find an ideal position with great pay. But this is also true for many more experienced workers.

Remember that small employers are where the action is. The Endicott Report from Northwestern University reports that small- to mid-sized companies tend to be the most active recruiters and large companies do less hiring. Smaller organizations are often more open to letting you take on new projects and directions. This openness allows many people to take one job and advance more rapidly to better ones.

Many students recognize that they must take control of their careers and make their own decisions. More than 8 out of 10 students surveyed in a Right Management Associates Career Expectations and Attitudes Comparison cited their own interests and skills as the major influence on their career choice. Other traditional influences, including family pressure, anticipated salary, and luck or chance, have dropped significantly in importance. When you interview for a position that matches your personality and talents, your natural enthusiasm for that job goes a long way in impressing interviewers.

An advantage that many younger people have is being more comfortable with newer technologies than their elders are. This important advantage helps many younger workers gain an edge over their older, but less technology-oriented, competitors. If you fall into the "not enough experience" category, stress any technical expertise you've acquired in school and emphasize the adaptive skills you identified in chapter 2 that would tend to overcome a lack of experience.

> **Tip:** *Don't overlook acceptable experiences such as volunteer work, family responsibilities, education, training, or anything else that you might present as legitimate activities in support of your ability to do the work you feel you can do.*

Again, consider expressing a willingness to accept difficult or less desirable conditions as one way to break into a field and gain experience. For example, indicating that you are willing to work weekends and evenings or are able to travel or relocate may appeal to an employer and open up some possibilities.

Issues Related to Women

Women have made great progress in many career fields, and many more employers, managers, professionals, and other workers in responsible positions are women than ever before. Even so, some employers and some career areas present barriers to women that are different than for men.

Despite the fact that the numbers of women in the workforce have increased rapidly, employers still imagine or experience problems. Here are some comments expressed in a survey conducted by the Society of Human Resource Management:

- "Working women with children have difficulties finding adequate child care in our area. Time off and absenteeism are big issues for our working mothers."

- "Gaining coworker acceptance of women in nontraditional roles is a serious problem. Many of our executives are uncertain how to manage women."

- "We have more women managers, but few women officers, and none on the board of directors. The glass ceiling is a reality."

Child Care

Unlike women, men are not likely to be asked about their child care issues prior to being hired and are far less likely to experience sexual harassment or gender-related discrimination or prejudice. Interestingly enough, women employers are often just as concerned as male employers are about a woman's family status. Employers of both genders assume that a woman is more likely to have child-related problems and want to be certain that these problems will not become a work-related problem.

A *Harvard Business Review* study documented that "on average, working mothers put in an 84-hour work week between their homes and their jobs; working fathers put in 72 hours, and married people with no children put in 50." Those numbers are staggering: A mother essentially holds down two full-time jobs. In addition, the care of elderly parents generally falls on the shoulders of women in our country. For women with or likely to have children or elderly parents, the number one task is to assure the interviewer that they don't intend to abandon their families but do intend to devote the necessary time to the job.

Again, handling questions about child care is simply a matter of turning the situation into a positive. Why not present your resourceful nature by giving an example of how you secured reliable child care? Or illustrate your management skills by describing how you handled work responsibilities when your child was ill and you needed to be at home. Be prepared to back up your loyalty claims with actual numbers of days missed from previous jobs.

Don't make the mistake of assuming that just because a woman interviews you, you don't need to bring up the child care issue. Even though she may be in the same boat herself, empathy rarely plays a role in landing you a position in a competitive job market. An interviewer's main focus is hiring someone who can do the job—regardless of whether they are a man or a woman.

Status Issues

It seems almost laughable that with the number of women in today's workplace, some interviewers would still be uncertain how to manage women. However, sensational headlines of sexual harassment and discrimination have trickled down to all levels of an organization. According to Carol Price, an educator and lecturer with Career Track who specializes in giving power presentations for women, you should begin establishing your equal status the second you walk in the room. "Once you do that, I really believe gender issues go away," she says.

So how do you "establish equal status" without appearing like a militant on a mission—another image of women that frightens employers? Simply look like you belong at the interview. "That means my head is held up, my shoulders are back, I walk in without hesitation, and I put my hand out," says Price. The handshake in particular is crucial. "A handshake was originally devised to prove we were weaponless. In a job interview, that translates to 'you and I are equal in value' when my hand goes out," Price says.

During the interview itself, do not complain about or even mention the lack of opportunity for women at your current or last job as the reason you are seeking new employment. Don't bring up the fact that there may be questions about your competency at all. Assume you are accepted and you will be, Price advises.

Issues Related to Men

Although this topic is seldom discussed, men also face certain biases because of their gender. Men are expected to have steady employment and not take time off for raising a family or caring for older parents. Those who do not aspire to higher status can be quickly branded "losers." You will also find few males in occupations dominated by women, such as grade school teacher, clerical worker, and nurse. Although some would argue that this condition is a result of these jobs paying poorly and having low status, it is clearly not always the case. Just as with women (but in different ways), men are expected to behave in certain ways, take on certain responsibilities, and quietly accept the limitations imposed on them.

In the recent past, many men have been frustrated in their inability to move up in pay and stature. Some big reasons for this are the large number of male baby boomers who are competing for the limited number of management jobs and the greater number of educated and qualified women in the workforce who want the same things. Higher percentages of women are graduating from high schools and from colleges now than men, and some experts predict that this change will result in long-term reductions in earnings of men compared to women. As a result, the competition for jobs has become tough.

Even so, there are few situations where being a man will work against you, particularly if you have a good work history. For example, how many men get questions about their plans to have or care for children or the possibility that they will make a move from the area because their wife takes a more prestigious job in another city? I know that I've never been asked about these issues in past employment interviews.

Sexual Preference

Sexual preference is an issue for some employers, and unmarried men and women may create suspicion as to their sexual preference in some interviewers' minds. Employers' fears are twofold. First, employers do not want their workplace to become a stage for airing social concerns to the detriment of producing products or services. The Society for Human Resource Management reveals that its respondents said, "We have not encountered any pressures from gay/lesbian groups directly. However, employees continue to voice their concerns about having to work with these groups and the potential risk—real or perceived—that they pose," and "In our traditional, conservative culture, managers have deeply ingrained biases and fears of gay and lesbian employees."

91

Another concern has to do with money. Rapidly increasing health-care costs are a serious problem for most organizations. Some employers are concerned about being forced to insure domestic partners because this could substantially increase their health-care costs. And, let's face it, some employers don't want to hire someone with a higher potential for HIV-related costs or simply do not want gay people on their staff.

Although I have advocated directly attacking stereotypes in other categories, I advise gay people to adopt the military's "don't ask, don't tell" policy related to this issue. The risks of divulging such personal information are too great to bring up in an interview, and your sexuality is not something you should have to discuss in a job interview anyway.

Racial or Ethnic Minorities

The largest minority groups in this country are African-American and Hispanic, although there are many smaller groups of recent immigrants, Native Americans, and others. The issue here is discrimination. The good news is that most employers fairly consider hiring a person based on his or her qualifications. Many employers go out of their way to give minorities fair consideration and actively recruit minorities.

The problem is that some employers are less likely to hire a qualified minority based on negative stereotypes. Unfortunately you are not likely to know which employers are being fair and which are not. Wondering why you are not getting a job offer will drive you nuts, so my best advice is the following:

- Assume that the interviewer is being fair and will consider hiring you based on your skills and abilities.

- In the interview, be yourself and focus on the skills you have to do the job. I give this same advice to everyone because following this procedure is important.

- Consider what stereotypes an employer might have and make sure you present details about your situation that would disprove them.

Limited English proficiency is a problem for many employers, and you will need to address this issue if it applies to you. Suggest that you are a good worker and are learning English rapidly, and consider how your language skills would allow you to help the employer provide better service to those who speak your native language.

Disability-Related Issues

Biases against those with disabilities are common enough that the government passed the Americans with Disabilities Act to prevent unfair discrimination. But negative assumptions about people with disabilities are the true barrier you are up against in the interview, no matter how many government agencies exist to back up your eligibility.

According to a Society for Human Resource Management survey, many respondents indicated that accommodating employees with disabilities presents difficulties for their organizations. Here are some specific comments:

- "We are a small organization, and accommodation of physical requirements for disabled workers and time off for illness and medical treatment cause disruption to work and schedules."

- "Some disabled workers are looked upon with disdain by their managers and peers. We have to overcome these attitudes."

I assume you will not seek a job that you can't or should not do. That, of course, would be foolish. So that means you are seeking a job that you are capable of doing, right? That being the case, you don't have a disability related to doing a particular job at all. The employer will still use his or her judgment in hiring the best person for the job, and that means people with disabilities have to compete for jobs along with everyone else. That is fair, so you need to present a convincing argument to employers for why they should hire you over someone else.

Most importantly, don't assume that the person chatting with you understands the technical details of your handicap. I see nothing wrong in casually mentioning how you have worked around your disability in other positions. Just remember to remain matter-of-fact in your explanation. If you avoid a defensive tone at all costs, you will not only put the interviewer at ease but also assure him or her that your future colleagues will admire your abilities and attitude, too.

Technology has provided opportunities to overcome disabilities in the workplace that you should become aware of. For example, speech-recognition software allows those who find keyboarding challenging (such as those with arthritis or other conditions that affect hand and wrist activity) to enter information

> **Tip:** *For more help on overcoming your disability in your job search, see the book* Job Search Handbook for People with Disabilities *by Daniel J. Ryan, Ph.D. (JIST Publishing).*

into a computer, and magnification features in operating systems such as Windows allow those with visual challenges to more easily read text on a computer screen. You can use these low-cost options to overcome potential challenges to your disability on the job.

Some Other Tricky Questions

Most employers avoid asking sensitive questions in a direct way. Instead, they ask indirect questions during the interview in hopes of finding out what they are not "allowed" to ask more directly.

The questions that follow are all legal, and they give you the opportunity to let an employer know that you and your situation will not be a problem. Think about what might concern an employer regarding your particular situation and plan to cover this during your interview, even if you are not asked about it in a direct way. Your good answer to one of these questions gives you the opportunity to put an employer's real, but perhaps unstated, concern to rest.

- **What would you like to accomplish during the next ten (or five) years?** Talk about what you want to do for that employer, not for yourself. "I'd like to cut production costs by at least 5 percent and find ways to streamline the layout procedure so that we can add publications without adding staff," is a much better answer than "I'd like to be making 25 percent more in salary and have my own magazine."

- **How long have you been looking for another job?** Never give an actual timeframe! Casually reply, "Time isn't a factor because I'm searching for the position that best matches my skills and goals."

- **What type of person would you hire for this position?** Flashback: You're casting your ballot for class president and mark the box for your opponent out of modesty. In doing so, you lost then, and you'll lose now if you don't choose yourself! "I'd hire someone who, beyond a shadow of a doubt, has the skills and people experience to handle this job. I would definitely hire myself."

- **Why do you want to leave your present job (or past jobs)?** Do not, under any circumstances, complain about your past jobs or employers. Doing so will make you seem negative and appear to be someone who is likely to have problems in a new job. More appropriate answers include this being a step in your career plans or wanting a better job location. "After introducing a more nutritious menu plan to the day care center and establishing a fun yet informative healthy lifestyle program for the after-school crowd, I've reached the top of the ladder at this smaller firm. I want the opportunity to use my expertise and continue to grow in a larger organization."

- **How do you normally handle criticism?** Ah, an easy question if you take it on the chin well. However, most of us aren't that admirable, and we have to put a twist on this common question. "Obviously, criticism comes from not doing the job properly, and I'm eager to correct any mistakes or misunderstandings the minute they arise. I'm grateful to the person who cares enough to help me out in that respect."

- **How do you feel about working overtime and on weekends?** Even if this job prospect does not appeal to you, this question can be answered so that your response does not harm you. "I have no problem devoting evening hours and weekends to getting a special project done. I also believe that a balanced life leads to a fresh, energetic employee who is less likely to burn out, so I try to pace myself for a consistent, dependable job performance over the long run, too."

- **What do you do for fun in your spare time?** This question has a dual motivation. First, the interviewer is confirming your response to the "Will you work overtime?" question. If you replied "yes" to that question, but then outline a lifestyle that involves weekends at a cabin, evenings at the gym, and commitments to various nonprofit and community events, it's unlikely you'll cancel those plans to work overtime. On the other hand, this is also an opportunity for the interviewer to confirm those things he or she can't legally ask, such as if you have a family, if you attend church, and so on. "My in-laws have a cabin by a nearby lake, and the children enjoy going there on weekends. I accompany them when I can, but sometimes work-related projects prevent that. Of course, the grandparents welcome those times so they can spend one-on-one time with the kids."

- **Describe your typical day.** Naturally, leave out the fact that you aren't a morning person or you start winding down at 4:30 p.m. to hit the parking lot by 5:00 p.m. Use this opportunity to advertise how well you organize yourself and conceptualize long-term projects. "I keep a calendar on my desk with appointment times recorded on the left side and tasks to accomplish that day on the right. I allot time each day to stay in touch with other departments and to return any missed phone calls or e-mail promptly. Overall, my entire day is focused on providing customers with a top-notch product."

- **What do you like most about your present boss?** For most candidates, finding something nice to say in response to this question is not too hard. Focus your answer on the type of supervision your boss provides and not necessarily on a personality type. "I appreciate the regular feedback" is a more useful response than "I enjoy the fact that he/she always has an upbeat attitude," even though both are certainly positive answers.

- **What do you like least about your present boss?** You knew this question was coming based on the previous question. Again, stick to management principles and skip the personality conflicts. Interviewers also like to pose the "What do you like best/least about your present job?" set of questions as well. As I have advised before, continue to look at your current job's opportunities rather than specific unappealing tasks. "I don't like to type my own memos" is honest, but short-sighted.

Interview Techniques Employers Use to Psych You Out

Employers today are all too aware of the costs associated with hiring the wrong person, so they want to be sure they hire the best candidate. That desire can lead them to try to "trick" you into admitting background weaknesses, questionable ethics, and personal secrets that indicate you cannot handle the job. Although some interview techniques appear quite innocent, their effects can be deadly if you are unaware of what is happening.

Keep in mind, though, that turnabout is fair play. You can prepare for these devious interviewers by knowing what to do when subjected to scrutiny. As always, though, I do not encourage you to lie but to know in advance that your task in an interview is to emphasize your strengths, not reveal your weaknesses. If you have been honest in assessing your skills and have targeted a job that you feel confident about, you need only tell the truth and leave out all irrelevant information.

Although most interviewers will know less about interviewing than you (because you have read this book), some will be masters of the craft. Books have also been written to help professional interviewers, and one of my all-time favorites is entitled *The Evaluation Interview*. Written by Richard Fear (I just love the irony of his name), this book is a must-read for interviewers wanting to increase their ability to manipulate an unsuspecting job seeker. Following are some of Fear's suggested techniques for eliciting negative information. Learn to recognize them so they cannot be used to eliminate you from consideration.

- **Misleading facial expressions.** Just as you use your posture—leaning forward, smiling, good eye contact—to express interest, the inter-viewer may also attempt to guide your answers with facial clues. For instance, lifting the eyebrows a little and smiling slightly conveys that the listener is receptive and expectant—and that is all it takes to con-vince some people to divulge negative facts about themselves to their new "friend." This half-smile and raised eyebrows routine also takes the edge off a delicate or personal question. Don't be misled: You must still answer these sensitive questions with the careful wording you have rehearsed, no matter how concerned and nonjudgmental the interviewer appears.

- **The calculated pause.** Experienced journalists have long elicited information from hard-boiled criminals, slick-tongued politicians, and interview-savvy celebrities by using the calculated pause. The technique works even better on job applicants. Most of us are not comfortable with silence and rush to fill the void with verbal noise. Therefore, when the interviewer says nothing but maintains eye con-tact, most job seekers feel pressured into either giving more details to their answer or starting another topic altogether.

The best way to handle silence is by remaining quiet and appearing pleasant. This response creates a non-hostile standoff; and, in the interest of time, the interviewer eventually asks the next question. Most pauses are measured in seconds, and it is rare for more than two to pass without the interviewer realizing you have not fallen for this ploy. If you are compelled to say something, at least turn the tables. "I think that answers the question, unless there is something else you wish to know," forces the interviewer to become the respon-dent.

Red-Flag Words and Phrases

Here, according to Richard Fear, are the most common words or phrases an experienced interviewer might use to encourage you to give them negative information:

- To what extent did you...?
- How do you feel about/like...?
- Is it possible that...?
- How did you happen to...?
- Has there been any opportunity to...?
- To what do you attribute...?
- might...
- perhaps...
- somewhat...
- a little bit...

- **Direct and indirect questions.** Although you are not all that likely to run into many well-trained interviewers, they are out there. Experienced interviewers often use indirect language to encourage you to tell them more than you might if you were asked the same question more directly.

  During the course of an interview, keep your ears tuned for phrases such as "To what extent did you...?" "How did you feel about...?" and "Is it possible that...?" Fear calls these phrases "wonderful" and "remarkably effective" because they turn leading questions into open-ended ones. But don't be lulled into missing their sting: "To what extent were you successful on that job?" still carries the meaning of its harsher counterpart, "Were you successful on that job?" Keep your answer directed toward satisfying that unspoken question, and your value will jump in the interviewer's estimation.

- **Two-step interview questions.** Just as a dance partner leads you through a series of premeditated steps to complete a specific dance, so does the interviewer use questions that are designed to guide you into an overall pattern. The best way to do this is to introduce a general subject and then hone in on the reason for your answer. The method works like this: The interviewer leads off a round of questions with a query such as "What subject did you decide to major in?" He or she then comes back with "Why?"

Interviewers use the two-step method to probe for clues to your judgment, motivation, and other factors of your personality. So do not think you are completely off the hook with a smooth answer like "History, because I believe it ultimately holds the solutions to problems in the future." When you are in the hands of a master interviewer, he or she is likely to ask you why that aspect seems important to you or why that compelled you to spend four years devoted to it instead of just taking a course or two. The best way to perform the two-step is to be prepared before you ever enter the interviewer's office. The more you understand yourself, the more gracefully the two of you will dance.

- **Laundry-list questions.** Beware of questions that offer a variety of options from which to choose (the so-called laundry list). The interviewer is not always trying to help you think in a stressful situation. In fact, it is just the opposite. When interviewers throw out a question with a series of possibilities from which to select, they are often trying to confirm details they picked up from a previous comment you made. Richard Fear provides an example: Assume that you, the applicant, have dropped some hints that seem to indicate a dislike for detail. The interviewer can often follow up on such clues by including a reference to detail in the laundry-list question at the end of the discussion of work history.

- **Double-edged questions.** Another tricky technique interviewers use to probe a job seeker's weaknesses is the double-edged question. It is called this because you are asked to choose between a rock and a hard place: You won't choose the first option unless you have a high degree of skill or personality in that area; the second is phrased so that it is easy to choose it, even though it is the less desirable one. Ouch!

  Here is an example: "What about your spelling ability—do you have that ability to the extent that you would like, or is that something you could improve a little bit?" (Notice the liberal use of softening words thrown in for good measure.) If you select the first option, it implies you feel no need for improvement—and you had better be prepared to back that up with perfect spelling! The second choice invites you to confess you are not up to speed in this area. Your best answer to a double-edged question is to frame it in the context of your strengths. Here's a sample response: "Because I'm a perfectionist, my spelling ability probably will not ever be what I hope for, but I am an above-average speller. And I am very careful to check any words that I am not sure of so that no spelling errors remain."

Key Points: Chapter 5

- Think about the things in your background that an employer might interpret as a negative. Then make sure you have a response ready that will help turn that negative into a positive.

- Make a list of questions that will be difficult for you to answer. Review the list of questions at the end of chapter 4 and include any you find there that you need to work on.

- Use the Three-Step Process to answering interview questions used in chapter 4 to present your situation honestly and positively.

- Ask someone you know to ask you these difficult questions and practice answering them.

Chapter 6

Getting More Interviews

Although this book's focus is on improving your interviewing skills, you won't be able to put those skills to work unless you get interviews. That's why I have included this chapter. This short chapter describes the job search methods that I have found can substantially reduce the time required to get a job. The techniques go beyond traditional methods to show you how to land interviews before anyone else ever knows there's an opening. Although I have written more thorough job search books, the information in this chapter may be all you need to get a better job in less time.

The Four Stages of a Job Opening

Most jobs are filled before employers even need to advertise them. To find these opportunities, you have to get in to an employer before the job is made fully public. Here are the four stages of a job opening:

1. **There is no job open now.** Before a job is created or available, it obviously does not exist. If you asked an employer if he or she had a job opening at this stage, that person would say "No." Perhaps no openings are planned or all positions are occupied.

   In a conventional job search, there would be no basis for you to have an interview with this employer. Most job seekers completely ignore the opportunities that exist in this situation. Yet should an opening become available at any time in the future, those who are already known to the employer will be considered before all others. About 25 percent of all jobs are filled by people the employer knows of before the job is even open.

2. **No formal opening exists, but one or more insiders know of a possibility.** As time goes on, someone in an organization can usually anticipate a position becoming available before one actually opens up. It could be the result of a new marketing campaign or product, an increase in business, an observation that someone is not doing well on the job, someone who is thinking about relocating, or a variety of other things. It's not always the boss who knows first, either.

In previous jobs, I have often known that a coworker was looking for another job even though the boss did not. Or I wondered why a certain person didn't get fired. Typically, if you were to ask an employer if there were any job openings at this stage, you would be told "No" once again. And there is no job opening—yet. For this reason, most job seekers keep on looking, not realizing that a job opportunity is right before them. Unfortunately for them, about 50 percent of all jobs are filled by people whom the employer knows by this stage of an opening.

3. **A formal opening now exists, but it has not been advertised.** At some point in time, the boss finally says that, yes, there is a job opening and that the organization is looking for someone to fill it. However, with few exceptions, days or even weeks go by before that job is advertised in some public way. If you were to ask whether a job opening exists at this stage, you might still get a "No," depending on whom you ask.

   In larger organizations, even the human resources department doesn't get formal notice of an opening for days or even weeks after the opening is known to people who work in the affected department. In large organizations, people who work there often don't know of openings in other departments. In smaller organizations, of course, most staff would know of any formal openings.

   In any case, once a job opening finally reaches this stage, it is the first time a person using a conventional approach to the job search might get a "Yes" response to the question of whether any openings were available. About 75 percent of all jobs are filled by someone who finds out about the job before it leaves this stage.

4. **The job opening is finally advertised.** As more time goes by and a job opening does not get filled, it might be advertised in the newspaper or posted online, a sign may be hung in the window, career services are notified, or some other action is taken to make the opening known to the general public. At this stage, virtually every job seeker can know about the opening, and if the job is reasonably desirable, a thundering horde of job seekers will now come after it.

What the Four Stages Mean to You

As the previous section explained, you can be considered for a job opening long before a formal opening exists and long before it is advertised. Most jobs are never advertised because someone like you gets there before the job needs to be advertised. Employers don't like to hire strangers. They prefer to hire people they already know or who are referred to them by someone they know. Many are willing to talk to you even before they have a job opening if you approach them in the right way. Once you know each other, of course, you are no longer strangers.

About 25 percent of the people who get hired become known to the employer before a job opening exists. Another 25 percent or so of those who get hired find out about the opening during the second stage of a job opening. Jobs that are filled during the first and second stages of a job opening are simply not available to someone using traditional job search methods. Half of all jobs are filled by the time traditional search methods come into play.

The Most Important Job Search Rule of All

The four stages of a job opening make it clear that most jobs are filled before they are advertised. This pattern illustrates the most important job search rule of all:

> Don't wait until the job is open before asking for an interview!

The best time to search for a job is before anyone else knows about it. Most jobs are filled by someone the employer meets before a job is formally open. So the key is to meet people who can hire you before a job is available. For this reason, these jobs are sometimes referred to as the hidden job market or the networked job market. Instead of saying "Do you have any jobs open?" say "I realize you may not have any openings now, but I would still like to talk to you about the possibility of future openings." By using this simple approach, you will hear many employers say "Yes" instead of "No." Not all, but many.

The Most Effective Job Search Method: Warm Contacts

Salespeople who call on potential customers via phone or by dropping in without an appointment call this technique making *cold contacts*. In the job search context, cold contacts are job leads obtained from contacting people you don't know, employers in particular. In contrast, I use the term *warm contacts* to describe leads for job openings that come from people you already know. These warm contacts include friends, relatives, and acquaintances, and they are usually much more effective at getting you job leads and interviews than cold contacts are.

Making Warm Contacts

Job leads obtained from friends and relatives account for about one-third of all job leads. More recent studies that asked job seekers for lead sources other than friends or relatives found other groups such as "business associates" and "acquaintances" provided leads as well. All personal referrals together probably account for about 40 percent of the ways that people find jobs. That makes using personal contacts the most important job search technique of all.

Leads developed from direct contacts with employers are also very important. About 30 percent of all job seekers find their jobs using this method. Together, these two techniques—leads from people you know and direct contacts with employers—account for about 75 percent of all job leads. If you practice a little, getting leads from your warm contacts may be the only job search technique you need.

Identifying Hundreds of Warm Contacts with Three Steps

The people who know you are the same ones who are most likely to help you—if only they knew what to do. Yet few job seekers seem willing to ask for meaningful help from the people they know in developing job leads. If job seekers ask their friends, relatives, and acquaintances for help at all it is of the vague, "Tell me if you hear of anything" variety. Although this crude approach does work often enough, people you know—your warm contacts—can and will be much more helpful if you learn to ask them to help you in more specific ways.

Knowing that leads provided by warm contacts are the most effective source of jobs for most people, it makes sense to systematically develop these contacts. Yet few job seekers go about developing their warm contacts in an organized way. With just a few simple techniques, you might be amazed at how many people you know—or can get to know.

Step 1: List Contact Groups of the People You Know

You know far more people than you may at first realize, and many of them will help you uncover job leads that cannot be found in any other way. To determine just how many people you do know, begin by listing the *types or categories* of people you know:

- Friends
- Relatives
- Clients
- Former employers
- Former coworkers
- School friends
- Alumni lists
- Members of my political party—in and out of elected positions
- Members of my church
- Members of social, fraternal, or other clubs
- Present or former teachers
- People at my children's sports games/events
- Neighbors
- People in my athletic club
- People I play sports with
- Members of a professional organization I belong to (or could join)
- People who sell me things or provide me with professional services (insurance, hair salon, mechanic, shop clerks)
- People I play cards with

Step 2: Create Warm Contact Lists

Although most people agree that "you have to know someone to get a job," most job seekers often tell me they "don't know anyone." One of those assumptions is true; namely, that people very often *do* get jobs through someone they know. But job seekers are mistaken if they think they don't know people.

If I asked you to take the first group on your list (for example, "Friends,") and write a list that includes everyone you are friendly with or who is even somewhat friendly to you, how many people would you guess that would be? 10? 25? 200? Next, estimate how many people are in each of the other groups and note your estimate next to each entry on your list.

> **Tip:** *Some contact groups are ideal for making out-of-town contacts. For example, although you most likely do not personally know everyone who graduated from your school, an alumni list can help you locate past graduates who live all over the country. If you have a specific location you want to move to, you can contact alumni who live in that area and ask them to help you to locate job leads there; many will be willing to help you.*

When you are finished, don't be surprised if the number of people you know is larger than you anticipated. It's not at all unusual for someone to get hundreds of potential contact people this way. Some groups, such as people who belong to your religious group or who went to the same school, can be enormous. They don't all know about job openings, of course, but they are a place to start. Remember, each contact on your list is a source of potential job leads.

For each of the contact groups you listed previously, use a sheet of paper to make a separate list. Begin with friends and write as many friends' names on that list as you can think of. Then do the same thing for relatives. When you have completed these two lists, you should have a significant number of names of people who know you. In fact, these lists may be the only ones you need. You can save the other lists to do later in your job search.

Step 3: Use Your Warm Contacts to Develop an Expanding Network of Contacts

Armed with your lists of friends and relatives, you have the beginning of a larger list of people who, in turn, can refer you to others. Of course, some of the people on your lists will be more helpful than others. Keep in mind though that these people are the ones who will be most likely to want to help you. Many job seekers do not follow through with their warm contacts and do not get the job leads from these important contacts that they could.

The JIST Card®: A Mini-Resume and a Powerful Job Search Tool

JIST Cards are a job search tool that gets results. I developed JIST Cards many years ago, almost by accident, as a tool to help job seekers. I was surprised by the positive employer reaction they received back then, so I developed them further. Over the years, I have seen them in every imaginable format, and forms of JIST Cards are now being used on the Internet, in personal video interviews, and in other electronic media.

How Did JIST Cards Get Their Name?

In case you were wondering, the word *JIST* is an acronym originally created for a self-directed job search program I developed years ago. It stands for "Job Information & Seeking Training." The word *JIST* was later trademarked and has been used for many years now in various forms (including JIST Publishing) to identify self-directed job search, career, and other materials.

Think of a JIST Card as a very small resume. A JIST Card is carefully constructed to contain all the essential information most employers want to know in a very short format. It typically uses a 3-×-5–inch card format, but it has been designed into many other sizes and formats, such as a folded business card or part of an e-mail message.

Your JIST Cards can be as simple as handwritten or created with graphics and on special papers or electronic formats. You should create a JIST Card in addition to a resume because a JIST Card is used in a different way.

What matters is what JIST Cards accomplish—they get results. In my surveys of employers, more than 90 percent of JIST Cards form a positive impression of the writer within 30 seconds. More amazing is that about 80 percent of employers say they would be willing to interview the person behind the JIST Card, even if they did not have a job opening now. I know of no other job search technique that has this effect.

Writing Your JIST Card

A JIST Card is small, so it can't contain many details. It should list only the information that is most important to employers. To write your card, follow these steps:

1. **Type your name at the top of the card.** You can center it and use bold text to make it stand out, as you would on a resume.

2. **Give two ways for the employer to contact you.** Space down a few lines and left-align this information. Generally, all you will need to include is your daytime phone number or cell phone number and your e-mail address.

3. **Give a broad job objective.** Space down another line or two and left-align this information. A broad objective will allow you to be considered for many jobs.

4. **List your years of experience.** Space down again and add one sentence that summarizes how long you have been working in this field.

5. **Detail your education and training.** In the same paragraph, add a sentence that tells what degrees, certifications, diplomas, and other relevant training you have.

6. **Showcase your job-related skills.** Still in the same paragraph, add up to four sentences that tell what you can do and how well you can do it. Be sure to include accomplishments and numbers to support them. (See chapter 2 for more on identifying these skills.)

7. **State your availability and preferred working arrangements.** If applicable, space down and add a sentence that states any special availability you might have, such as "interested in part-time work," or "available with two weeks' notice."

8. **End with your key adaptive skills.** Space down a few more lines and add one last sentence that tells what personality traits you have that make you a good employee. (See chapter 2 for more on identifying these skills.)

> **Tip:** *JIST Cards are harder to write than they look, so carefully review the examples at the end of this section and use the content of your resume as a starting point for content.*

Using JIST Cards

You can use a JIST Card in many ways, including the following:

- Attach one to your resume or application.

- Enclose one in a thank-you note.

- Give them to your friends, relatives, and other contacts so that they can give them to other people.

- Send them out to everyone who graduated from your school or who is a member of your professional association.

- Put them on car windshields.

- Post them on the supermarket bulletin board.

- Send them in electronic form as an e-mail.

I'm not kidding about finding JIST Cards on windshields or bulletin boards. I've seen them used in these ways and hear about more ways people are using them all the time.

Formatting JIST Cards

JIST Cards are most often used in paper formats. Many office-supply stores have perforated light card stock sheets that you can run through your computer printer. These tear apart into 3-×-5–inch cards. Many word-processing programs have templates that allow you to format a 3-×-5–inch card size. You can also use regular size paper, print several cards on a sheet, and cut it to the size you need. Print shops can also photocopy or print them in the size you need. Get a few hundred at a time. They are cheap, and the objective is to get lots of them in circulation.

The following sample JIST Cards use a plain format, but you can make them as fancy as you want. Look over the examples to see how they are constructed. The content of the samples, and of your own JIST Card, can be adapted for use as e-mail attachments, as part of an online or other portfolio, and other formats. So be creative and adapt the idea to best fit your own situation.

> **Tip:** *Once you have your own JIST Card, put hundreds of them in circulation. JIST Cards work, but only if they get to the people in your network.*

Sandy Nolan

Position: General Office/Clerical

Message: (512) 232-9213

More than two years of work experience plus one year of training in office practices. Type 55 wpm, trained in word processing, post general ledger, have good interpersonal skills, and get along with most people. Can meet deadlines and handle pressure well.

Willing to work any hours.

Organized, honest, reliable, and hardworking.

Juanita Rodriguez

Message: (639) 361-1754
Email: jrodriguez@email.com

Position: Warehouse Management

Six years of experience plus two years of formal business course work. Have supervised a staff as large as 16 people and warehousing operations covering over two acres and valued at more than $14,000,000. Automated inventory operations resulting in a 30% increase in turnover and estimated annual savings of more than $250,000. Working knowledge of accounting, computer systems, time and motion studies, and advanced inventory management systems.

Will work any hours.

Responsible, hardworking, and can solve problems.

Using E-mail and the Phone to Contact Employers

The telephone and e-mail are important tools to use well in your job search. Let's first cover my thoughts on e-mail; then we can turn our attention to using the phone.

Contacting Employers by E-mail

E-mail is a wonderfully efficient way to communicate. It offers a variety of advantages that a phone cannot, including the following:

- **It's more convenient.** You can send e-mail any time you want, and the recipients can deal with the messages as they choose. An e-mail message does not interrupt people as a phone call can.

- **You can attach files.** You can attach a copy of your resume, JIST Card, or anything else you want.

- **You can forward it to others.** Your e-mailed resume or message can be easily forwarded by the recipient to others who might be interested, along with a note from him or her to consider you.

- **It's fast.** There are no delays as there are when mailing or transferring papers within an organization.

- **It's free.** You incur no long-distance phone charges and no mailing costs.

- **Some people prefer e-mail.** I am one of many who prefer getting work-related e-mail instead of phone calls in most situations. The reason is that phone calls interrupt what I am doing, but I can deal with e-mails in a more controlled and time-efficient way. I get so many phone calls from telemarketers and other nuisance calls that I will often let incoming calls whose numbers I don't recognize (via caller ID) go to voice mail. Many employers also prefer e-mail, particularly from people they don't know, and some will insist that you communicate with them only via e-mail.

You may also prefer to use e-mail yourself. Even so, I think you should primarily use the phone during your job search, for these reasons:

- **E-mail is easily ignored and deleted.** One of e-mail's advantages to the recipient is also its disadvantage to you. E-mail allows employers to ignore a message until they choose to deal with it. A busy person may wait days before responding, quickly view and put it aside for a "later" response, or simply delete it as junk e-mail from someone they don't know. Think of e-mail as a locked car sitting in your driveway. You don't think much about it until you want to use it.

- **Phone calls get a bit more attention.** A phone call, however, is more like a car alarm going off. It's far more likely to get your attention or at least get you to wonder why it is going off. E-mails can get attention, but you have to remember that most e-mail users get lots of junk mail and learn to quickly delete anything that looks like it comes from someone they don't know. Attachments to e-mail are particularly dangerous to open because they can contain viruses. So unless your e-mail is to someone you know, it has a good chance of being ignored or deleted. We all get junk phone calls too, of course, but almost everyone will at least listen to voice mail before deleting it, which is more attention than most e-mail gets. And calling someone presents the possibility of getting to that person in a more direct, personal way.

- **A phone call provides a different and more interactive experience.** If you prepare well, a direct phone contact allows you to have an impact that an e-mail simply can't. Even if you only get to the potential employer's voice mail, a well-done presentation will at least be listened to. If you do get through to the potential employer, a phone conversation allows you to interact with that person in a more personal and natural way. The employer hears your voice and can ask you questions in real time and get your responses, experiencing your verbal communication skills. An interactive phone call also allows you to react to what's being said and allows an employer to make a decision whether to see you in an interview or to follow up in some other way.

- **Saying no to you is harder on the phone.** Phone calls provide an experience that is closer to being face to face. It is a much more personal interaction and one where you both have the opportunity to interact, react to questions and tone of voice, and correct misunderstandings. If you ask the employer to set up a time to see you, you are also much more likely to succeed than you would be in asking the same thing in an e-mail. This assumes, of course, that the employer likes how you come across in the phone call.

Keep in mind that my objective is to help you to get interviews. Making direct contacts with employers is one of the most effective job search methods there is. E-mail is most effective when it's used intelligently and appropriately in combination with the phone techniques in the next section.

Using the Telephone to Get Interviews

Many people find the assertive phone techniques I present in this section intimidating. Most people worry about making such phone calls, and they find all sorts of reasons to avoid making them. True, making phone calls to people you don't know is more difficult than sending the same people e-mails. Why? Because e-mails are far less likely to result in a direct and personal situation where you would feel foolish and rejected. But is avoiding more challenging situations worth it if doing so prolongs your job search? I think not. So try to face your fears and let the logical part of you help overcome your resistance to using the phone.

Making these calls does require you to overcome some shyness. But once you get used to it, making direct contacts by phone is quite easy, and it is often necessary to effectively follow up on an initial contact you had to make by e-mail.

Using the telephone in combination with e-mail is one of the most efficient ways of looking for work. You don't spend time traveling, and you can contact a large number of people in a very short time. Once you learn how, you can easily make personal contact with more than 20 employers in one morning. Most phone calls take only a minute or so. And most employers don't mind talking to a person they might be interested in hiring.

To get yourself accustomed to making this kind of phone call, I suggest that you start by making calls to your warm contacts. Then call the people they refer you to. This network of people is often happy to help you. Even people you pick from the *Yellow Pages* will usually treat you well. The experience of thousands of job seekers is that very few potential employers will be rude to you. And after all, if you do encounter somebody who is rude, you probably wouldn't want to work for that sort of person anyway.

Job seekers get more interviews by using the phone than by any other method. For example, you can use the phone to

- Call people you already know to get interviews or referrals without delay.

- Follow up by calling leads you initially get from want ads or the Web, when the only initial contact provided is via e-mail.

- Stay in touch with prospective employers and with people in your network who might hear of openings.

- Make cold calls to employers whose names you get from the *Yellow Pages* and the Internet.

The simple-to-use phone techniques I describe in this section can make a big impact on how many job leads you get. Many people have used these methods to get two or more job interviews in just a few hours of work each day.

Creating an Effective Phone Script

Another use of your JIST Card is to use it as the basis for a phone script. You will learn more about how to do this in this section. Many job search programs use the phone script approach I present here, and the experience of the many thousands of job seekers who have used this approach has been that it takes from 10 to 15 cold-contact phone calls to get one interview. That may sound like a lot of rejection, but most people can easily make 10 to 15 calls in less than an hour. In two hours of making phone calls, most people in these programs get two or more interviews. How many job search methods are you aware of with that kind of a track record?

The phone script I have presented here assumes that you will contact a person who does not know you and who may or may not have a job opening. An example of this situation would be if you were making cold calls to organizations listed in the *Yellow Pages* or online.

As you gain experience making phone calls, you will adapt what you say to specific situations. (For example, you would want to adapt your phone script for use in calling people you know.) For learning purposes, I suggest you write and use your phone script in the specific way I outline below. This effective approach has been carefully crafted based on years of experience.

I have divided the phone script into five sections. As I review each section, complete the related section in the Phone Script Worksheet found later in this chapter.

1. **Introduction.** This one is easy. Just fill in your name on the Phone Script Worksheet. Write your name as if you were introducing yourself.

2. **The position.** Always begin your statement with "I am interested in a position as... ." It takes you only about 30 seconds to read your phone script, and you don't want to get rejected before

Tip: *Make certain that you have a carefully written JIST Card for yourself to use as the basis for writing your phone script. There are no shortcuts here, so go back and write your JIST Card and use that content for what follows.*

you begin. So don't use the word *job* in your first sentence. If you say you are "looking for a job" or anything similar, you will often be interrupted. Then you will be told there are no openings. For example, if you say "Do you have any jobs?" the person you are talking to will often say "No." And then your presentation will come to a screeching halt in less than 10 seconds.

Remember that in the new definition of an interview, you are not looking for a job opening; you simply want to talk to people who have the ability to hire a person with your skills even if they don't have a job opening at the present moment.

Fill in your job objective on the Phone Script Worksheet to complete the Position statement. If the job objective from your JIST Card sounds good spoken out loud, add it as is to your worksheet. If it doesn't, change it around a bit until it does. For example, if your JIST Card says you want a "management/supervisory position in retail sales," your phone script might say "I am interested in a management or supervisory position in retail sales."

3. **The strengths and skills statement.** The skills section of your JIST Card includes length of experience, training, education, special skills related to the job, and accomplishments. Rewriting the content from this part of your JIST Card for use in your phone script may take some time because your script must sound natural when spoken. You may find it helpful to write and edit this section on a separate piece of paper before writing the final version on your script worksheet. After completing this, you should read the final version out loud to hear how it sounds. You should read it to others and continue to make improvements until it sounds right.

4. **The good worker traits and skills statement.** Simply take your top adaptive skills, which you pinpointed in chapter 2 and are listed at the end of your JIST Card, and make them into a sentence. For example, "I am reliable and hardworking, and I learn quickly." These are some of the most important skills to mention to an employer, and putting them last gives them the greatest emphasis and may influence the employer to give you an interview.

5. **The goal statement.** The goal of the phone script is to get an interview. So I suggest that you be direct and use "When can I come in for an interview?" as your goal statement. The reason is that this assertive approach tends to work. If you say, for example, "May I

come in for an interview?" (or "Could you please, please, let me come in to talk with you?"), the employer has an opening to say "No." And you don't want to make it easy for the employer to say no. Employers can reject you without your help.

Use the Phone Script Worksheet to write out your final draft, but write rough drafts out on separate sheets of paper until you are satisfied with your script. In writing your phone script, consider the tips that follow:

- **Write exactly what you will say on the phone.** A written script helps you present yourself effectively and keeps you from stumbling while looking for the right words.

- **Keep your telephone script short.** Present just the information an employer would want to know about you and ask for an interview. A good phone script can be read out loud in about 30 seconds or less. This is about the same time it takes to read a JIST Card. Short is better!

- **Write your script the way you talk.** Your JIST Card is a good basis for a phone script, but it uses short sentences and phrases, and you probably don't talk that way. So add some words to your script to make it sound natural when you say it out loud.

- **Use the words I use.** As you write your phone script, avoid being too creative. Over the years I refined the words provided in the Phone Script Worksheet. In order to avoid specific problems, I suggest you use them as they are presented.

  For example, do not write or say, "Good morning, my name is _____" because that will build a bad habit, which you will realize all too late on one overcast afternoon. I have learned the best words to use through years of making mistakes, and there is no need for you to make the same ones. Start my way, and you can change it to your way after you have mastered mine.

- **Practice saying your script out loud.** I know that your neighbors may think you are nuts, but reading your script out loud and perhaps in front of the mirror etches it into your mind in a way that reading it to yourself cannot do. It has something to do with neural pathways and cognitive retrieval stuff. It also may be something more spiritual, having to do with the way we define ourselves. However, the fact remains that reading an honestly prepared phone script out loud helps you accept that all the good stuff your phone script says about you is true. Having this information etched into your subconscious also helps you in an interview.

PHONE SCRIPT WORKSHEET

Complete this worksheet with your final script content. It may take several attempts to get it to sound right, so use separate sheets of paper for your drafts before completing this form. Once you have it the way you want it, write your final script on this worksheet. Later, you can read this on the phone, just as you have written it here.

1. Introduction

Hello, my name is _____

2. The position

I am interested in a position as_____

_____

3. The strengths and skills statement

_____

_____

4. The good worker traits and skills statement

_____

_____

5. The goal statement

When can I come in for an interview?

Calling Employers Directly—Making Cold Contacts—to Find Job Openings

Now that you have developed your phone script, you need to know how to use it effectively. The first step is to identify companies to call. Try looking in the *Yellow Pages* under a category of businesses or organizations that need people with your skills. Just call them up and ask for the person in charge. Many people have used this type of cold contact to obtain interviews that would have been difficult to get any other way. Another approach is to use the want ads or Internet job listings to identify employers who might hire someone like you. For example, you may find that Metro Hospital is hiring maintenance workers. But you want to be an office worker. Could you call them? Yes, you could. You could contact the person hiring maintenance workers via e-mail or phone and ask for the person you should speak with about office jobs.

The most important thing to remember is that when you are cold calling an organization, your goal is to get directly to the person who is most likely to supervise you so that you have an opportunity to use your script. Most organizations have someone who answers the phone or an automated system to handle incoming calls. In both cases, the function of these systems is to screen incoming calls and get them to the correct person. But both of these systems can also screen you out, particularly if you don't have the name of the person you need to talk to. So here are some tips to increase your chances of getting to the person most likely to hire you. They have been refined over many years, and they work!

- **Talk to a real person if you can.** You can get through most automated answering systems if you have the name of a specific person. If you don't, most such systems have an option that allows you to push the zero button or do something else to talk to the receptionist. Once you get through to the operator or receptionist, understand that this person is busy and will try to quickly screen your call. A receptionist's task is to either refer you to someone who can help you or to block your call from bothering anyone at all. Be nice to this person and ask for what you want.

- **Ask the receptionist to give you the name you need.** If you don't have the name of the person you need to speak to, ask for it. For example, ask for the name of the person in charge of the accounting department if that is where you want to work. Usually, a receptionist will give you the supervisor's name, and your call will be transferred to him or her immediately.

> **Tip:** *When you do get the name of a supervisor or manager, get the correct spelling and write it down right away. Then you can use the name in your conversation and can later send that person follow-up mail with his or her name spelled correctly.*

- **Ask for the person by title.** Depending on the type and size of the organization you're calling, you should have a pretty good idea of the title of the person who would be likely to supervise you. In a small business, you might ask to speak to the manager. In a larger organization, you would ask for the name of the person who is in charge of a particular department.

- **Avoid mentioning that you're looking for a job.** If you tell the receptionist you are looking for a job, he or she may transfer you to the human resources department (if the company has one) or ask you to send a resume or come by and complete an application. Unless you want to work in the human resources department, you probably don't want to talk with someone there. If the receptionist will not give you a manager's name or transfer you to the person you want, say thanks and end your call.

- **Try e-mail.** The Web sites of most organizations often list employee names and responsibilities. You can also send an e-mail to any Web address you can find for the company and ask for the name of the person in charge of the area you want. I've sent questions to Web managers or the general information address for the organization and had all sorts of questions answered. Write well and be pleasant and professional because e-mail is often forwarded to the person you are trying to reach. If one e-mail does not get you the response you want, try another e-mail to someone else at the organization.

- **Say that you are mailing something to the manager.** If the receptionist won't connect you with a hiring manager, end the call and call back another day. Tell the receptionist that you are getting ready to send some correspondence to the manager of the department that interests you. This is true, because you will be sending the manager something soon. Say you want to use the person's correct name and title. This approach usually results in getting the information you need. Say thank you and call back in a day or so. Then ask for the supervisor or manager by name. You will usually get through to the person this way.

- **Call during lunch or after hours.** If the receptionist is still screening you out, try calling when that receptionist is out to lunch. Other good times are just before and just after normal working hours. Less-experienced staff members are likely to answer the phones at that time and put you through. Plus, the boss might be in early or working late when the more experienced receptionist is not there to screen you out.

> ### *What Recruiters Do That You Can Do for Yourself*
>
> People who earn their living by finding talented workers for employers do a lot of cold calling and e-mailing. They call lots of employers to find out their needs and then look for people who can fill those needs. They do this by defining a need and creating a sense of urgency to fill it. In a similar way, your task is to create this need for the employer and fill it with you and your skills.
>
> Recruiters know that most employers will almost always consider hiring good people. They know that there may not be a job opening now, but there may be one in the future for a good person. So they find out what is ideally needed, and then try to find someone that matches that need. If they succeed, they earn a fee.
>
> You can do the same thing by learning as much as you can about an organization and then going after the needs of that organization. If they are growing rapidly and you think you can help them, tell them how you would do this. Get to the people in that targeted organization and present the skills you have that will help them solve specific problems.

Calling People You Know—Making Warm Contacts—for Job Leads

Previous examples in this chapter involved cold contacts to employers, where no one referred you. Learning how to make these cold contacts is important, because they can be effective. Cold calls are also difficult for many people, so learning specific techniques eases the process and, I hope, encourages you to make more cold calls.

Even though cold calls are often effective, being referred by someone the employer knows is almost always better. Here are some tips for making these sorts of "warm contact" calls:

- **Tell the employer your connection.** If you have been referred by someone, immediately give the name of the person who suggested you call. For example,

  "Hello, Ms. Beetle. Joan Bugsby suggested I give you a call."

  If the receptionist asks why you are calling, say:

  "A friend of Ms. Beetle suggested I give her a call about a personal matter."

  When a friend of the employer recommends that you call, you usually get right through. It's that simple.

- **Adapt your phone script to the situation.** Sometimes, using your telephone script does not make sense. For example, if you are calling someone you know, you would normally begin with some friendly conversation before getting to the purpose of your call. Once you have chatted informally for a while, you can get to the purpose of your call by saying something like this:

"The reason I called is to let you know I am looking for a job, and I thought you might be able to help. Let me tell you a few things about myself. I am looking for a position as… (continue with the rest of your phone script)."

You will encounter other situations that require that you adjust your script. Use your judgment. With practice, it becomes easier!

Asking for the Interview

The primary goal of a phone contact is to get an interview. To increase your chances of getting an interview, you need to practice **asking** for the interview. To succeed, you must be ready to get past the first and even the second rejection. You must practice asking three times for the interview! The following exchange demonstrates how you can do this.

Ask once:

> **You:** When may I come in for an interview?

> **Employer:** I don't have any positions open now.

Ask again:

> **You:** That's OK; I'd still like to come in to talk to you about the possibility of future openings.

> **Employer:** I really don't plan on hiring within the next six months or so.

Be prepared to ask again:

> **You:** I appreciate that you are busy, so I'll only ask for half an hour or so of your time. I'd like to come in and learn more about what you do. I'm sure you know a great deal about the industry, and I am looking for ideas on getting into your field and moving up.

Although this approach does not always work, asking the third time works more often than most people would believe. You must learn to keep asking after the first time you are told no. Of course, you should be sensitive to the person you are speaking to and not push too hard, but most job seekers face the problem of not being persistent enough rather than being too aggressive. Employers often assume that a person who overcomes their objections will show the same persistence on the job.

> **Tip:** *If the employer agrees to an interview, you should arrange a specific time and date. If you are not sure of the employer's correct name or spelling, call back later and ask the receptionist. Also be sure to get the correct address for the interview.*

Ending the Phone Call in Other Ways

Sometimes you will decide not to ask for an interview during your phone call. The person may not seem helpful, or you may have caught him or her at a busy time. If so, you can do other things to make the most of the call:

- **Get a referral.** Ask for names of other people who might be able to help you. Find out how to contact them, and then add these new referrals to your job search network. When you call them, remember to tell them who referred you.

- **Ask to call back.** If an employer is busy when you call, ask whether you can call back. Get a specific time and day to do this and add the call to your "to-do" list. When you do call back (and you must), the employer is likely to be positively impressed. People respect the professionalism of people who keep their word and may give you an interview for just that reason.

- **Ask if you can keep in touch every week or so.** Maybe the employer will hear of an opening or have some other information for you. Many job seekers get their best leads from a person they have checked back with several times.

Key Points: Chapter 6

- Appointments with prospective employers who might have a job in the future or who can give you the name of someone else who might have a current or future opening count as an interview.

- Aim to get two interviews each day you are looking for a job.

- The best sources for job leads and interviews are the people you already know. Your friends, family, and acquaintances also can introduce you to or give you the names of other people who may have job leads.

- Three good methods of contacting employers are JIST Cards, e-mail, and the phone. These methods work best when used together, but the phone is the most important and effective job search tool.

- Using a prepared phone script is essential to effectively asking for interviews over the phone.

Chapter 7

Following Up After the Interview

The interview has ended, you made it home, and now it's all over, right? Wrong. Effective follow-up actions can make a big difference in getting a job offer over more qualified applicants.

What to Do as Soon as You Get Home

Following up can make the difference between being unemployed or underemployed and getting the job you want fast. When you get home from the interview, do the following:

- **Make notes on the interview.** While it is fresh in your mind, jot down key points. A week later, you may not remember something essential.

- **Schedule your follow-up.** If you agreed to call back next Monday between 9:00 a.m. and 10:00 a.m., you are likely to forget unless you put it on your schedule.

- **Send your thank-you note.** Send the note the very same day if possible. Send an e-mail thank-you that day, and follow this with a thank-you note through regular mail.

- **Call when you said you would!** When you call when you said you would, you create the impression of being organized and wanting the job. If you do have a specific question, ask it at this time. If a job opening exists and you do want it, say that you want it and explain why. If no job opening exists, say you enjoyed the visit and would like to stay in touch during your job search. If interviewers referred you to others, let them know how these contacts went. Ask them what they suggest your next step should be. This would also be a good time to ask, if you have not done so before, for the names of anyone else with whom you might speak about a position for a person with your skills and experience. Then, of course, follow up with any new referrals.

- **Schedule more follow-up.** Set a time to talk with this person again. And, of course, send the interviewer another thank-you note or e-mail.

The rest of this chapter details several ways to follow up with employers after the interview.

The Importance of Thank-You Notes

Resumes and cover letters get the attention, but thank-you notes often get results. Sending thank-you notes makes both good manners and good job search sense. When used properly, thank-you notes can help you create a positive impression with employers that more formal correspondence often can't.

Three Times When You Should Definitely Send Thank-You Notes—and Why

Thank-you notes have a more intimate and friendly social tradition than formal and manipulative business correspondence. I think that is one reason they work so well—people respond to those who show good manners and say thank you. Here are some situations when you should use them, along with some sample notes.

1. Before an Interview

In some situations, you can send a less formal note before an interview, usually by e-mail, unless the interview is scheduled for a fairly distant future date. For example, you can simply thank someone for being willing to see you. Depending on the situation, enclosing a resume could be inappropriate. Remember, this note is supposed to be a sincere thanks for help and not an assertive business situation. You could, however, enclose a JIST Card (see chapter 6). This note also serves as a way to confirm the date and time of the scheduled interview and as a gentle reminder to the recipient that you will be showing up at that time.

2. After an Interview

One of the best times to send a thank-you note is right after an interview. Here are several reasons why:

- Doing so creates a positive impression. The employer will assume you have good follow-up skills as well as good manners.

- It creates yet another opportunity for you to remain in the employer's consciousness at an important time.

- It gives you a chance to get in the last word. You get to include a subtle reminder of why you're the best candidate for the job and can address any concerns that might have come up during the interview.

- If the employer has buried, passed along, or otherwise lost your resume and previous correspondence, a thank-you note and enclosed JIST Card provide one more chance for that person to find your number and call you.

> **Tip:** *Send a thank-you note by e-mail or regular mail as soon as possible after an interview or meeting. This time is when you are freshest in the mind of the person who receives it and are most likely to make a good impression.*

For these reasons, I suggest you send a thank-you note right after the interview and certainly within 24 hours. The following is an example of such a note.

August 11, 20XX

Dear Mr. O'Beel,

Thank you for the opportunity to interview for the position available in your production department. I want you to know that this is the sort of job I have been looking for, and I am enthusiastic about the possibility of working for you.

Now that we have spoken, I know that I have both the experience and skills to fit nicely into your organization and to be productive quickly. The process improvements I implemented at Logistics, Inc., increased their productivity 34%, and I'm confident that I could do the same for you.

Thanks again for the interview; I enjoyed the visit.

Sara Smith

(505) 665-0090

---

3. Whenever Anyone Helps You in Your Job Search

Send a thank-you note to anyone who helps you during your job search. This group of people includes those who give you referrals, people who provide advice, or those who are supportive during your search. The following figure shows an example of this type of note.

October 31, 20XX
2234 Riverbed Ave.
Philadelphia, PA 17963

Ms. Helen A. Colcord
Henderson and Associates, Inc.
1801 Washington Blvd., Suite 1201
Philadelphia, PA 17963

Dear Ms. Colcord,

Thank you for sharing your time with me so generously yesterday. I really appreciated talking to you about your career field.

The information you shared with me increased my desire to work in such an area. Your advice has already proven helpful—I have an appointment to meet with Robert Hopper on Friday.

In case you think of someone else who might need a person like me, I'm enclosing another resume and JIST Card.

Sincerely,

Debbie Childs

Seven Quick Tips for Writing Thank-You Notes

Use these tips to help you write your thank-you notes.

1. Decide Whether E-mail or Regular Mail Makes More Sense

Consider the timing involved and the formality of the person and organization you're sending it to. If you need to get a letter out quickly because it has to arrive before an interview that's coming up soon, or if it's a thank-you note after an interview and you know the employer will be making a decision soon, e-mail is your best bet. Use regular mail if there's no rush and if you sense that the other person would appreciate the formality of a business letter printed on nice paper and received in the mail.

2. Use Quality Paper and Envelopes

Use good quality notepaper with matching envelopes. Most stationery stores have thank-you note cards and envelopes in a variety of styles. Select a note that is simple and professional—avoid cute graphics and sayings. A blank card or simple "Thank You" on the front will do. For a professional look, match your resume and thank-you note papers by getting them at the same time. I suggest off-white and buff colors.

3. Handwritten or Computer-Printed Is Acceptable

Traditionally, thank-you notes were handwritten, but most are computer-generated and -printed these days. If your handwriting is good, writing them is perfectly acceptable and can be a nice touch. If not, they can be word-processed.

4. Use a Formal Salutation

Don't use a first name unless you've already met the person you're writing to and he or she has asked you to use first names or you're writing to someone in a young, hip environment. Instead, use "Dear Ms. Smith" or "Ms. Smith," rather than the less formal "Dear Pam." Include the date.

5. Keep the Note Informal and Friendly

Keep your note short and friendly. Remember, the note is a thank-you for what someone else did, not a hard-sell pitch for what you want. Make sure, though, that in a thank-you note after an interview you give a subtle, gentle reminder of your skills or other qualifications that are relevant to the job. This hint lets the thank-you note serve as not only an expression of appreciation but also as a chance to get the last word on why you should be hired. The more savvy members of your competition will be doing this, so you had better do it, too.

Also, make sure your thank-you note does not sound like a form letter. Put some time and effort into it to tailor it to the recipient and the situation. As appropriate, be specific about when you will next contact the person. If you plan to meet soon, still send a note saying that you look forward to the meeting and say thank-you for the appointment. And make sure that you include something to remind the employer of who you are and how to reach you, because your name alone may not be enough to be remembered.

> **Tip:** *Always send a note or e-mail after an interview, even if things did not go well. It can't hurt (unless, of course, it's full of typos).*

6. Sign It

Sign your first and last names. Avoid initials and make your signature legible (unless you're being hired for your creative talents, in which case a wacky-looking, illegible signature could be a plus!).

7. Send It Right Away

Write and send your note no later than 24 hours after you make your contact. Ideally, you should write it immediately after the contact while the details are fresh in your mind.

More Sample Thank-You Notes

Following are a few more samples of thank-you notes and letters. They cover a variety of situations and provide ideas on how to structure your own correspondence. Notice that they are all short and friendly and typically mention that the writer will follow up in the future—a key element of a successful job search campaign.

Also note that several of these candidates are following up on interviews where no specific job opening exists yet. Getting interviews before a job opening exists is a very smart thing to do. All of these examples came from David Swanson's book titled *The Resume Solution* (with minor adjustments to include fictitious e-mail addresses) and are used with permission.

April 22, 20XX

Dear Mr. Nelson,

Thank you so much for seeing me while I was in town last week. I am grateful for your kindness, the interview, and all the information you gave me.

I will call you once again in a few weeks to see if any openings have developed in your marketing research department's planned expansion.

Appreciatively,

Phil Simons

Voice mail: (633) 299-3034

E-mail: psimons@email.com

September 17, 20XX

Mr. Bill Kenner
Sales Manager
WRTV
Rochester, MN 87236

Dear Mr. Kenner:

Thank you very much for the interview and the market information you gave me yesterday. I was most impressed with the city, your station, and with everyone I met.

As you requested, I am enclosing a resume and have requested that my former manager call you on Tuesday, the 27th, at 10 a.m.

Working at WRTV with you and your team would be both interesting and exciting for me. I look forward to your reply and the possibility of helping you set new records next year.

Sincerely,

Anne Bently
1434 River Dr.
Polo, WA 99656
Pager: (545) 555-0032

October 14, 20XX

Dear Bill,

I really appreciate your recommending me to Alan Stevens at Wexler Cadillac. We met yesterday for almost an hour, and we're having lunch again on Friday. If this develops into a job offer, as you think it may, I will be most grateful.

Enclosed is a reference letter by my summer employer. I thought you might find this helpful.

You're a good friend, and I appreciate your thinking of me.

Sincerely,

Dave

July 26, 20XX

Dear Ms. Bailey,

Thank you for the interview for the auditor's job last week.

I appreciate the information you gave me and the opportunity to interview with John Petero. He asked me for a transcript, which I am forwarding today.

Working in my field of finance in a respected firm such as Barry Productions appeals to me greatly. I appreciate your consideration and look forward to hearing from you.

Sincerely,

Dan Rehling
Cell phone: 404-991-3443

May 21, 20XX

Mrs. Sandra Waller
Yellow Side Stores
778 Northwest Blvd.
Seattle, WA 99659

Dear Ms. Waller:

Thank you so much for the interview you gave me last Friday for the Retail Management Training Program. I learned a great deal and know now that retailing is my first choice for a career.

I look forward to interviewing with Mr. Daniel and Ms. Sobczak next week. For that meeting, I will bring two copies of my resume and a transcript, as you suggested.

Enclosed is a copy of a reference letter written by my summer employer. I thought you might find it helpful.

Sincerely,

Elizabeth Duncan

Follow-Up Letters

After an interview, you might wish to send some follow-up correspondence in order to solve a problem or to present a proposal. I have already shown you some examples of thank-you letters and notes that were sent following an interview. In some cases, a longer or more detailed letter would be appropriate. The objective of this type of letter is to provide additional information or to present a proposal.

In some cases, you could submit a comprehensive proposal that would essentially justify your job. If there were already a job opening available, you could submit an outline of what you would do if hired. If no job were available, you could submit a proposal that would create a job and state what you would do to make hiring you pay off.

How to Use E-mail and Regular Mail for Thank-You Notes and Follow-Up Letters

Many hiring managers prefer correspondence via e-mail. It's easy, free, and instantaneous. Therefore, if the timeline on hiring is short, e-mail would have an advantage over regular mail.

When you are interviewed and the employer gives you his or her card with an e-mail address, corresponding via e-mail is generally acceptable. However, if you have a formal cover letter or thank-you note template and send these as e-mail attachments, make sure they are in a universal format such as Microsoft Word, WordPerfect, Rich Text, Adobe PDF, or HTML. Always mention the format of your letter in your e-mail message. If you are ever in doubt about whether an employer can open your attachments, you should directly type (or copy and paste) the cover letter or thank-you note into the body of your e-mail.

Although the regular mail service has improved considerably since the Pony Express days, it still takes a day or two to send and receive a thank-you note locally. Although a mailed letter often looks more formal than an e-mail letter, it may not be received in time for consideration. Consider the advantages and disadvantages of each method. Essentially it boils down to speed versus formality.

In writing such a proposal, you must be specific in telling the hiring manager what you would do and what results these actions would bring. For example, if you proposed you could increase sales, how would you do it and how much might profits increase? Tell employers what you could accomplish and they may just create a new position for you. It happens more often than you probably realize.

Whatever the situation, your post-interview letter should present any concerns the employer may have had with you during the interview in a positive light. For example, if the employer voiced concern over a lack of specific experience, you would address his or her concern by stating that you are a quick study, self-motivated, and detail-oriented. Once you have put the employer's concerns to rest, reinforce your interest in the job (if you are sending a post-interview letter). Include a statement like, "After hearing more about the job, I am even more certain my skills and education will be beneficial to your company. I am eager to begin working for you and will call next Tuesday to inquire about the hiring decision."

Follow-Up Phone Calls

Although you don't want to become a pest, most employers are favorably impressed with a job seeker who follows up by phone. Most job seekers are not nearly as assertive as they should be in staying in touch with an employer following an interview. Use these tips to improve your results when following up with phone calls:

- **Ask when would be a good time to call.** Before you leave the interview, ask when would be a good time to call back and note that time on your schedule.

- **Phone when you said you would.** Call back on the day and at the time the interviewer suggested. By then, if you do as I suggest, he or she will have received your thank-you e-mail and note. This will likely create a good impression, as will your calling back.

- **If there is an opening, ask for it.** If you want the job, say so. Tell the interviewer why you want it and why you think it is a good fit for you.

- **Be brave; call back on a regular basis.** If the employers you are meeting with don't have an opening now, ask to stay in touch. Make it clear that you are interested in working for them and would like to call or e-mail them back on a regular basis to see how things are developing. This kind of contact will keep you in their minds. As positions come up that fit your skills, these employers are more likely to consider you before they advertise the job. But this will happen *only* if you stay in contact with them on a regular basis!

- **Ask for referrals.** Each time you contact employers, ask whether they know of anyone else who might have a job opening for someone with your skills. If not, ask whether they can give you names of others to contact to see whether they have openings.

Key Points: Chapter 7

- After an interview, write down important items from the interview, plan your follow-up, and start writing your thank-you notes.

- Whether sent through e-mail or regular mail, thank-you notes are a friendly and effective way to demonstrate your good manners and create a positive impression in the minds of employers.

- In some situations, you may want to send a follow-up letter to provide the employer with more information, present a proposal, or clear up any issues that came up in the interview.

- Staying in touch with an employer by phone can be a good way to ask for the job you want, find out about future opportunities, and get referrals to other potential employers.

Chapter 8

Negotiating Your Salary

Few job seekers are prepared to discuss their pay requirements prior to a job offer or to negotiate it well after a job offer is made. As a result of their blunders, many job seekers are eliminated from consideration during the selection process without even knowing why. Others who do get a job offer too often mishandle the discussion of pay in a way that results in their being paid less than they might have received—or losing a job offer they might have accepted.

The fact is that most people don't negotiate their salaries at all because few know how to negotiate effectively. At one time or another, each of us has probably failed at this process. Most job seekers accept the first offer thrown their way because they're afraid that negotiating will kill any chances to get the job. I personally never attempted to negotiate a salary package during the early years of my career because nodding politely and saying "That's fine" was the path of least resistance. But in today's economy, that passive acceptance can cost us more than we can afford to lose.

Negotiation experts cite four strategic mistakes that novice negotiators often make. Although these mistakes refer to negotiations in general, they are often at the root of salary negotiation problems as well.

1. **Lack of persistence.** Herb Cohen, author of *You Can Negotiate Anything,* told *USAir* magazine, "People present something to the other side, and if the other side doesn't 'buy' it right away, they shrug and move on to something else. If that's a quality you have, I suggest you change it. Learn to hang in there. You must be tenacious."

2. **Impatience.** As Michael Schatzki, owner of the New Jersey–based Negotiation Dynamics warns, "The impatient negotiator has two strikes against him. He's not willing to let the process work itself out, and he's not willing to be deadlocked for a while and see what happens. And time often is the key to successfully concluding a negotiation."

3. **Going in too low.** All too often one side in the negotiation process accepts in advance a settlement that is lower than the other side had

in mind. Once a low position is revealed, an experienced negotiator is unlikely to go higher.

4. **Lack of research.** Few people are prepared with facts to back up their position in negotiations. They go on "feel" to establish a value. Lack of preparation can be a very expensive mistake.

Farr's Four Rules of Salary Negotiation

To avoid these problems, I've developed four basic rules of salary negotiation that you should keep in mind.

Early Pay Discussions Can Screen You Out

Early in the traditional screening process, many employers want to know how much you expect to be paid. Before the interview, they may seek this information on applications and in want ads. And some employers ask you how much you expect to earn very early in the interview process.

Just why is this information so important to them? The reason is that many employers don't want to waste their time with people who have salary expectations far above what they are willing to pay. Put simply, they want the information so that they can screen you out.

Employers look for ways to eliminate as many people as possible during the early phases of a traditional interview process. There may be many applicants for an opening, particularly if the job was advertised or is reasonably attractive in some way. Employers will try to find out whether you want more money than they are willing to pay. If so, they figure that, if hired, you may soon leave for a better-paying job. That is the reason for my first rule regarding salary negotiations.

> *Farr's Salary Negotiation Rule #1*
> Never talk money until after an employer decides he or she wants you.

Discussing salary early in the interviewing process is not to your advantage. Your best position is to use techniques that are likely to satisfy a curious employer without giving a specific dollar amount. Here are a few ways you could respond to an initial interview inquiry about your pay expectations:

- "What salary range do you pay for positions with similar requirements?"

- "I'm very interested in the position, and my salary would be negotiable."

- "Tell me what you have in mind for the salary range."

- "I am interested in the job and would consider any reasonable offer you might make."

"Employers are anxious to know how your joining the organization will impact their bottom line, and they'll try to get to the subject as soon as possible," says Doug Matthews, Executive Vice President of Career Transition Services for Right Management Associates, an executive outplacement firm. Salary issues are the main reasons candidates are knocked out of the running during the screening process, according to outplacement industry surveys. Responding appropriately to salary questions can get you past screening interviewers, who rarely have authority to negotiate salaries, and in front of decision-makers with whom the real negotiations take place.

So always defer the question as many times as you have to until you are sure it's the real thing and not just part of a screening process. Then, when the timing is right, maneuver the interviewer into naming the starting point. Just remember the most important rule of salary negotiations: The one who speaks first loses.

With a bit of luck, stall tactics such as these will get the employer to tell you the salary range or at least delay further discussion until later, when it matters. If that doesn't work and the employer still insists on knowing your salary expectations, there are still some things you can do.

Know the Probable Salary Range in Advance

Approaching an interview without being prepared for discussions of pay is not wise. Although you will have to do a bit of research, knowing what an employer is likely to pay is essential in salary negotiations.

Farr's Salary Negotiation Rule #2

Know in advance the probable salary range for similar jobs in similar organizations.

The trick is to think in terms of a wide *range* in salary, rather than a particular number. Keep in mind that larger organizations tend to pay more than smaller ones, and various areas of the country differ greatly in pay scales. Find out the general range that jobs of this sort are likely to pay in your area. That information is relatively easy to obtain; all it may take is asking those who work in similar jobs, finding the information online, or visiting the library. See "Sources of Information on Pay for Major Jobs" at the end of this chapter for tips on finding this information.

Bracket the Salary Range

Let's assume that you have done your homework and you know a range that you are likely to be offered for a given job in your area. And let's also assume that you run into an interviewer who insists on knowing how much you expect to be paid. If this happens, I suggest negotiation rule #3.

Farr's Salary Negotiation Rule #3
Always bracket your stated salary range to begin within the employer's probable salary range and end a bit above what you expect to settle for.

Even if you have a good idea of how much a job might pay, you can easily get trapped into making a very costly mistake. Suppose that the employer is expecting to pay someone about $25,000 a year. Your research indicates that most jobs of this type pay between $22,000 and $29,000 a year. Let's also assume that you have run into an interviewer who insists on you revealing your pay expectations in the first interview.

You want to be a clever negotiator, so you say you were hoping for $30,000. You figure that stating that number will make the interviewer think you are not an easy target and will encourage him or her to make a higher offer later. Wrong. In many cases, saying this amount will probably eliminate you from consideration.

If you say you would take $22,000, one of two things could happen:

1. You could get hired at $22,000 a year, probably making that response the most expensive two seconds in your entire life.

2. The employer could look for someone else, because you must be worth only $22,000, and he or she wants someone who is worth more.

Once again, questions about pay during the early phases of the interviewing process are designed to help the employer either eliminate you from consideration or save money at your expense. You could get lucky and name the salary they had in mind, but the stakes are too high for me to recommend that approach. Your best bet is to be informed! See "Sources of Information on Pay for Major Jobs" later in this chapter for tips on figuring out the correct salary range for the position.

In my example, you figured that the probable range for the salary would be from $22,000 to $29,000. That is a wide range, but you could cover it by saying

> "I was looking for a salary in the mid- to upper twenties."

This response avoids mentioning a specific salary, and it covers a wide range.

If you were an employer and someone responded this way, how might you react? Most employers take a moment to consider the response and, after doing so, often conclude that your range is the same one that they are considering. The particular number the firm has in mind just happens to be $25,000, and your response "brackets" that figure. The impasse is over, and you can both get on with the interview. You win, and they don't lose.

You can use the same strategy for any salary bracket you may be considering. For example, if you want $28,000 a year and their range is $25,000 to $33,000, you could say "A salary in the mid-twenties to low thirties." The same bracketing techniques can be used with any salary figure.

Talking in terms of a salary range that extends a bit above what the employer was likely to consider often results in one of two positive outcomes:

1. If you are offered the job, you are likely to be offered more than the employer may have originally been willing to consider.

2. It gives you the option of negotiating your salary when it matters most—when the employer has offered you a job.

Don't Say No Too Soon

Too often, people lose the ability to negotiate salary because they mishandle the job offer or its discussion. This brings me to rule #4:

Farr's Salary Negotiation Rule #4

Never say no to a job offer either before it is made or within 24 hours afterward.

Many job seekers mishandle discussions of pay early in the interview process. They may not even realize that their response eliminated them from further consideration. That is why you should avoid discussion of pay if at all possible until a firm job offer is being made. Later in this chapter, I'll cover what to do when a job offer is being made. But, for now, it is important that you understand that discussion of pay before a job offer is made is a trap that can easily result in your being eliminated from being considered.

But what can you do if an employer insists on your stating your pay requirements early in the interview? Going back to the original example, you had decided in advance that you wanted to earn about $25,000 a year. Using the bracketing technique correctly, you say you would accept offers in the range from the mid- to upper twenties. In response, the interviewer then tells you that the organization wants to pay about $23,000. Because that is below what you had hoped for, you display some subtle signs of dis-appointment. The interviewer just might notice that reaction and decide to keep looking for someone who would be delighted with the $25,000 the organization wants to pay. If you had just had a bit more patience, you might have made a good fit. Perhaps that lost job would have turned out to be just the sort you had been looking for—a very nice job in all respects except the salary.

Had you handled things differently and not acted disappointed, you might have continued a pleasant chat, and the interviewer would have gotten to know you as the wonderful person you are. She or he just might have been able to come up with a few thousand more, having discovered you were worth it.

To avoid losing the job before the interview is over, you might consider countering a lower-than-hoped-for offer by saying something like this:

> "That is somewhat lower than I had hoped, but this position does sound very interesting. If I were to consider this offer, what sorts of things could I do to quickly become more valu-able to this organization?"

Or you might say that you would be happy to get more specific about salary later, after you have both gotten to know each other better.

I hope you now see why you should not negotiate your pay too early in an interview. Only later, when employers want you, are wages an appropriate topic. Remember that a discussion of salary is not necessarily a job offer. More often, it is an attempt to screen you out of consideration.

How to Delay Discussion of Pay Until It Matters

As my first rule of salary negotiation states, you should never discuss money until the employer indicates he or she wants to offer you a job. Yet employers use a host of ways to discover your acceptable salary early in the process, and thus force you to speak about money first. Classified ads are notorious for demanding that respondents list their salary requirements. If you feel that a particular ad is a good bet, indicate that your salary requirements are open to negotiation. Some cover letters go so far as to state that the subject shouldn't prove to be a barrier to a "mutually satisfactory relationship"—a phrase I think appropriate if you think you may be overqualified for the job.

Next, an employer may try to trick you on the standard job application. Almost all of these forms have blanks that not only ask what salary you are expecting, but what salary you previously made. Doug Matthews of Right Management Associates says, "In many cases, your most recent earnings may not be relevant to the value of the new position. Scope of responsibility, the organization's culture and size, risk, location, industry segment, and competition can vary greatly." Fill in the blank concerning current expectations with the word *negotiable* and enter "confidential pending employment" in the spaces for your previous salaries.

Never, ever mention a dollar figure until you are sure you're talking to the decision-maker and not a go-between. Only the person you will work for directly has the power to accept or reject your requests and make counteroffers. Be assured that interviewers will attempt to wangle salary information from you early in the screening process. The question often is phrased in a casual tone and comes in many forms. The pressured candidate's natural response to any direct question is to volunteer information (in this case, a dollar figure). Instead, practice your answers to the common salary questions in the following sections.

What Is Your Current Compensation?

Tom Jackson, author of *Interview Express,* offers this reply: "In my last job, I was paid below the market price for my skills. I was willing to accept this for a while because it gave me the opportunity to learn and develop. Now I am very clear about the value I can offer to an employer and I want my salary to be competitive."

If you feel this type of answer does not reflect your situation, smile and politely reply, "I didn't realize we were ready to discuss salary so soon. I'd feel more comfortable tabling this subject until we are both sure we have a fit."

Another effective tactic, which Richard Germann and Peter Arnold recommend in their book *Job and Career Building* (which is now out of print, but available through interlibrary loan or as a used book on www.amazon.com and other Web sites), is to offer a future-oriented salary figure. The conversation would run something like this: "The job you have described, if carried out in a superior manner, should be worth about $30,000 in three or four years." Most employers don't hesitate to agree because you are talking about a time in the future to work up to that figure. After you reach an agreement, say, "Because we agree that the job will be worth $30,000 in three or four years, I'm content to leave the starting salary up to you. What do you think would be a reasonable figure?" According to the same book, demonstrating your high performance and income expectations motivates the interviewer to offer a reasonable starting figure.

What Are Your Salary Requirements?

Doug Matthews of Right Management recommends replying: "Compensation is an important issue. However, my goal is to explore positions that allow me to maximize my strengths and solve significant challenges within an organization. I'm looking for a strong fit between my skills and specific company needs. When that happens, I'm certain the compensation issue will fall into place. Could you give me an idea of the range you've established for this position?"

If the interviewer provides a range, remain quiet for a few seconds; then say that the upper end of the range is in your ballpark and that you would like to learn more about the position's responsibilities. Notice that you did not agree to anything.

Should the interviewer push for salary requirements, Matthews advises parrying, "I understand the need to discuss specific compensation requirements. However, it might be more effective for me to know how your organization values this position. I'm certain you have ranges for various levels within the organization that are fair, based on experience, responsibility, and contribution. I'd be pleased to work within those ranges. If this is a new position, I'd like to discuss your needs further. Then I might be able to provide a proposal that would help us arrive at an appropriate compensation figure."

Yes, that answer is a mouthful. If you believe that type of answer is too complex for your needs, simply say, "I hesitate to disclose compensation figures because this position contains elements that may differ from my recent position. We may be comparing apples and oranges. Let's table this subject until we're both more comfortable with making an employment offer."

How Much Do You Need to Live On?

This appears to be such an innocent and caring question on the surface. Don't be fooled: A literal answer is not in your best interest, as it takes the focus away from how much you are worth and concentrates instead on whether you could do better with your finances. Unfortunately, some employers will use any information you provide to your disadvantage.

Online Salary Negotiation Help

You have that job offer in hand—now how can you be sure that you negotiate the salary you deserve? Get inside information and tips at Quintessential Careers' Salary Negotiation Tutorial (www.quintcareers.com/salary_negotiation.html). You'll find tips on getting the best possible salary, turning unacceptable offers into acceptable ones, handling salary discussions during an interview, and more. You'll also find useful articles on negotiation techniques. You can take an online quiz to see how your negotiating techniques stack up and follow links to other salary-negotiation guides.

Job seekers who press for more money based on their personal needs or wants rather than their value to an employer often create a bad impression. The employer might think "Why should I believe that you are responsible and stable if you have financial problems of your own making?" or "My dream of traveling Europe is just as important as your desire to buy a fishing boat." The most sensitive employers may try to help you find ways to reduce your living expenses by suggesting cheaper restaurants, lower-rent apartments, loan-consolidation services, and so on. Remember, you are dealing with a virtual stranger, and asking this person to sympathize with your personal value judgments is completely inappropriate. Instead, base a vague answer on your ability to do the job. Haldane's example: "I can be quite flexible if I have to be. Money isn't my highest priority. But I feel I have quite a lot to offer to an organization like yours. I'd like my salary to be based on my value to you. I'm sure you have a fair income structure for this kind of job—how much do you have in mind?"

What to Say When an Offer Is Made

Serious negotiation often begins only after you've been invited to several interviews. When some employers are ready to make an offer, they come right out and say, "We'd like to offer you the position provided we can come to a salary agreement." Again, let the employer open up the bidding. The employer is likely to make a very low offer or a reasonable one. The following sections explain what you should say in each situation.

The Offer Is Not What You Want

Remember my salary negotiating rule #4? It was "Never say no to a job offer either before it is made or within 24 hours afterward." At the point in time when the employer is offering you the job, you need to keep this rule in mind. Never, never turn down a job offer in an interview!

Let's say that you get a job offer at half the salary you expected. Avoid the temptation to turn it down there and then. Instead, say:

> "Thank you for your offer. I am flattered that you think I can do the job. Because this decision is so important to me, I would like to consider your offer and get back with you within two days."

Leave and see if you change your mind. If not, call back and say, in effect:

> "I've given your offer considerable thought and feel that I just can't take it at the salary you've offered. Is there any way that I could be paid more, in the range of _____?"

Even as you say no, leave the door open to keep negotiating. If the employer wants you, he or she may be willing to meet your terms. It happens more than you might imagine. If the employer cannot meet your salary needs, say thank you again, and let him or her know you are interested in future openings within your salary range. Then stay in touch. You never know.

> **Tip:** *Do not reject a job offer to try to get a higher wage. Understand that once you reject an offer, the deal is off. You must be willing to lose that job forever.*

The Offer Is Reasonable

Just as you shouldn't reject an offer too quickly, take time to think about accepting a job, too. Accepting a reasonable offer right away can be a mistake. Germann and Arnold list the following considerations that many people ignore in the rush to accept or reject a job offer:

- Is the job description (duties, responsibilities, and authority) clear?

- What is the employer's attitude toward advancement?

- Who will you be working with?

If you don't have a straight answer yet for these questions, don't make a move you could regret. Instead, keep plugging away until the picture comes into clear focus.

Also, discussing the offer with others before saying yes is often wise. Here is one way to delay until you can give the offer some thought:

> "Thank you for the offer. The position is very much what I wanted in many ways, and I am delighted at your interest. This decision is an important one for me, and I would like some time to consider your offer."

Ask for 24 hours to consider your decision and, when calling back, consider negotiating for something reasonable. A bit more money, every other Tuesday afternoon off, or some other benefit would be nice if you can get it easily. However, if you want the job, do not jeopardize obtaining it with unreasonable demands. If your request causes a problem, make it very clear that you want the job anyway.

They Offer, You Want It—Now It's Time to Negotiate!

The employer you've spent the past two weeks wooing has opened the bidding with a lukewarm figure—one that would certainly pay your bills and yet is somewhat below what you feel you are worth. But exactly how should you ask for more? You aren't a professional athlete with a savvy manager to wheel and deal the details, and isn't the time limit on this opportunity short?

Knowing Your Price

At this stage of the game you're in tune with industry standards and local pay ranges and have correctly "encouraged" the interviewer to name the opening dollar figure. But there's one final ingredient you must have squared away before you make a counteroffer: How much cash and fringe benefits will it take to make you accept the position?

> **Tip:** *Always heed the advice Tom Jackson dishes out in* Interview Express: *Negotiations should never be angry or emotional, no matter how much pressure there is on either side. Assert your value so that the employer will view you as a highly worthwhile addition rather than as someone who is overpriced.*

Michael Schatzki, owner of the New Jersey–based Negotiation Dynamics, recommends that you know your worst case or Least Acceptable Settlement (LAS) and your best possible result or Maximum Supportable Position (MSP). You come up with these numbers through your research on the industry and a serious study of your personal financial position. Plan to start the bidding at your MSP, but should the offer fail to rise above your LAS, continue job hunting.

Playing the Negotiation Game

As *Job and Career Building* points out, the first number the interviewer mentions is rarely the highest possible salary offer. But in the spirit of the negotiating game, you can't blurt that out to the person on the other side of the table. So when that initial salary figure is mentioned, your first reaction must be silence. According to authors Richard Germann and Peter Arnold, your silence signals two things:

1. You are carefully considering the offer.

2. You are not satisfied with it.

Words at this moment weaken your position because they require the interviewer to defend his or her offer. In fact, Haldane Associates has discovered that in more than 50 percent of all situations where silence is used, the interviewers cough up a higher figure without further discussion!

However, when a better offer isn't immediately forthcoming, one of two things will happen: The interviewer will either explain the offer or ask for your reaction. In the first instance, the *Job and Career Building* authors recommend you listen politely but continue your thoughtful silence as long as necessary. In the latter case, indicate that you are enthusiastic about the job, but the offer is on the modest side. Then suggest continuing the discussion at another meeting—the following day, if possible.

Unfortunately many job candidates interpret this tactic as "playing hard to get." Haldane Associates scoffs at this label, and so should you. In fact, this consulting firm has interviewed a number of employers who have stated that employees who handle themselves well during their salary negotiations were treated with greater respect and given more opportunities to advance within the organization.

Ending the Negotiation

Several clues tip you off to the fact that the employer has extended its best possible salary package. If the same figure is repeated after a day or two break, chances are good it won't change. Perhaps the employer may begin tossing in additional benefits without changing the figure, again signaling that the price is firm.

Once your salary has been decided, begin hashing out these areas:

- Stock options
- Vacation time
- Performance bonuses
- Flexible time (work four 10-hour days and take Fridays off; work 10 a.m. to 6:00 p.m. to avoid rush hours; job-share; or telecommute)
- Parking privileges
- Company car
- Geographic location, if there is more than one office

According to the International Association of Corporate and Professional Recruiters, Inc., financial incentives, equity opportunity, and geographic location rank as the top three

Tip: *Whether or not you are satisfied with the salary eventually settled upon, don't forget Haldane Associates' most valuable advice: Always ask for a commitment to review your salary in six months, based on your demonstrated value.*

motivating factors respectively in evaluating a job offer. Time flexibility, health insurance policies, and maternal/paternal leave policies ranked fourth through sixth.

Before you shake hands to seal the deal, ask for 24 hours to think it over. Such careful thought and responsible consideration can only be viewed as professional and will earn the respect of a potential employer.

Sources of Information on Pay for Major Jobs

You have already learned a variety of good techniques for negotiating your pay, but their effective use assumes that you know in advance the prevailing pay scale for the jobs you want. Although you often won't know precisely how much a particular employer might pay, some quick research will often give you a good idea.

The Top Excuse for Avoiding Research

When asked to relate the number one mistake job candidates make during the negotiation process, most employers say it is a failure to prepare. For those job seekers who take the time and effort to investigate salary ranges and benefits rather than simply "winging it," the rewards are worth every second of research. This section gives you a handle on where to locate such information quickly and painlessly.

The reasons individuals give for failing to prepare for salary negotiations, such as, "I didn't realize the subject would come up so quickly and didn't have time to prepare" or "I could tell the interviewer wasn't going to budge, and I didn't want to blow the opportunity," can often be boiled down to one excuse: Most of us are uncomfortable putting a dollar value on our skills.

"The reason many of us are hesitant to take our foot off the brake, get off our butts, and let people know who we are and what we do well is because we feel it is tasteless and unprofessional to do so," says behavioral scientist George Dudley. "We reached that conclusion because the people who have done it in the past are so oily. 'If I have to be like them to do that,' the logic runs, 'then I don't want to do it.'" Michael Schatzki of Negotiation Dynamics has an even more colorful way of describing job seekers' lack of enthusiasm for salary negotiations. "They see it as high stakes, table-pounding, your worst nightmare of a used-car salesman, and it all seems negative," he comments.

In the business world, modesty will get you nowhere. There is nothing shameful about asking for the amount of money you are worth. In today's environment, knowing yourself and your capabilities is a valuable commodity in itself.

Sources of Information on Salary and Wages

Like other parts of the job search process, the key to salary negotiations is preparation. It is very important for you to do your research before you begin negotiations. In order to determine the salary you are willing to accept, investigate the salary range someone with your skills and experience can expect to receive. The following sections describe some of the best sources of information.

The Internet

Use the sites in this section (from *Best Career and Education Web Sites* by Rachel Singer Gordon and Anne Wolfinger) to learn the average pay rates in your chosen field and find cost-of-living information for different parts of the country.

- **www.careerOINK.com** (powered by JIST Works): This Web site provides free information, including more than 14,000 job descriptions and average pay for major jobs. Keep in mind that the pay ranges are national averages; local rates can differ significantly and those with less than average experience typically earn less.

- **Abbott, Langer & Associates (www.abbott-langer.com):** You can find free summary data, including median salaries, from the various salary surveys that Abbott, Langer & Associates conducts. This site contains current statistics for more than 450 benchmark jobs and from more than 8,000 participating organizations. Select from major fields, such as accounting, information technology, and engineering, and then choose from the surveys available for each field.

- **JobStar Salary Information (jobstar.org/tools/salary/):** You can jump directly to JobStar's more than 300 links to general and profession-specific salary surveys and also take some time to explore salary negotiation strategies and test your own salary IQ. Information on print resources you might want to check out is also included. The site links to California libraries, but you can look up these books in your own local public library.

- **The Salary Calculator (www.homefair.com/calc/salcalc.html):** Thinking about relocating for a job? Compare the cost of living among hundreds of U.S. and international cities with this handy salary calculator. Just enter your salary and current location, and then select another city to find out what you'll need to make there to sustain the same standard of living. While here, check out other relocation tools as well.

- **Salary Expert (www.salaryexpert.com):** Find free regional salary reports by selecting your job title and then your ZIP code or city. Reports list the position's average salary, benefits, and bonuses; show how salaries in a given area compare to the national average; provide a brief description of the occupation; give the average cost of living in the area; and list links to salary info for related jobs. Also available at this site are selected feature articles and international salary reports.

- **Wageweb (www.wageweb.com):** Although Wageweb is geared toward employers needing to know competitive wages in order to retain employees, individuals can also find useful salary information at this site. It provides national salary information for more than 170 benchmark positions, broken down by category and then by job title.

Reference Books

Your local library or bookstore should have a number of references to help you determine the salary range for the occupation you are considering. A list of such references follows. Ask your librarian for assistance, as most libraries provide a variety of references that may not be listed here.

- **The *Occupational Outlook Handbook* and *America's Top 300 Jobs*** (JIST Works). Both books contain the same text and are updated every two years based on information from the U.S. Department of Labor. I mentioned these books in chapter 3 as an important source of information on jobs. Both include starting and average pay rates for the most common jobs. You can use detailed information from these books to know what pay to expect for various jobs at differing levels of experience.

- *Career Guide to America's Top Industries* (JIST Works). This book includes information on about 60 major industries. Written mainly for job seekers, it provides a description of each industry, employment projections, working conditions, typical occupations, training and advancement, outlook for industry growth, and earnings information.

As this book shows, there can be substantial earnings differences among industries, even for the same types of work. Knowing about these differences in advance is important so that you are not unpleasantly surprised. On the other hand, you can also benefit from your industry research by looking for jobs in industries that tend to pay better.

- *College Majors Handbook with Real Career Paths and Payoffs* (**JIST Works**). This book is based on an enormous study of 150,000 college graduates by the U.S. Census Bureau. The authors used this information to create a practical guide on the actual jobs and earnings of college graduates in 60 majors. The result is the most accurate facts available on long-term outcomes associated with particular majors.

- *Best Jobs for the 21st Century* (**JIST Works**). This helpful book provides pay rates, job descriptions, and many other details for about 500 major jobs that have the best combination of pay, projected growth, and number of job openings.

- *American Salaries and Wages Survey* (**Gale Group**). This title gives detailed information on salaries and wages for thousands of jobs. Data is subdivided geographically. It also gives cost-of-living data for selected areas, which is very helpful in determining what the salary differences really mean. Finally, it provides information on numbers employed in each occupation, along with projected changes.

- *American Almanac of Jobs and Salaries* (**Avon Books**). This title provides information on wages for specific occupations and job groups, many of which are professional and white collar. It also presents trends in employment and wages.

Professional Associations

Virtually every occupation and industry you can imagine (and some that you can't) has one or more associations. Most of the larger ones conduct salary surveys on an annual basis, and this information is available to members and, sometimes, in their publications. Back issues of an association's journals or newsletters (if you can get them) can provide excellent information on trends, including pay rates. Consider joining an association to get access to this information, as well as access to local members with whom you can network. You can search for associations by industry and geographic location at the American Society of Association Executives Web site at www.asaenet.org/cda/asae/associations_search/. Choose Gateway to Associations to locate an association.

Local Information

Local pay rates can differ substantially from national averages; starting wages are often substantially less than those for experienced workers; some industries pay better than others; and smaller organizations often pay less than larger ones. For these reasons, you need to find out prevailing pay rates for jobs similar to those you seek. Following are some additional sources of this information:

- **Your network:** Talk to colleagues in your professional network. Although people frequently don't want to tell you what they personally are making, usually they are willing to talk about salary ranges. Ask colleagues, based on their experience, what salary range you might expect for the position.

- **Job search centers:** These centers (which you can find in schools, libraries, and community centers or as part of federal, state, or local government programs) frequently keep salary information on hand.

- **Your past experience:** If you are applying for a job in a field in which you have experience, you probably have a good idea of what someone with your skills and abilities should be paid. Think about your past salary. Unless the job you are applying for requires a dramatically different amount of responsibility than your former position, your previous salary is definitely a starting point for negotiations.

Key Points: Chapter 8

- Avoid discussing salary until after an employer offers you a job. If the employer insists on having a number, offer a salary range.

- Don't accept or reject a job offer right away. Take a day to think about it, and make sure you have the information you need to make your decision.

- Let the employer name a salary first, and then you can negotiate up from there.

- Prepare yourself for salary discussions by researching salaries for the position you are applying for. Be sure to find as much local information as possible because pay varies widely depending on location.

I hope you found the advice in this book helpful. If you have suggestions for the next edition, let me know. And let me know how things turn out in your interviews. You can contact me through the publisher via e-mail at info@jist.com.

Appendix

Online Interviewing and Job Search Resources

The Internet has a wealth of information that you can use to support your interviewing and job search efforts. Here are some of the most helpful sites I've found.

Interviewing Tips

Interviewing Success
www.collegegrad.com/intv/

Job-Interview.net
www.job-interview.net

Monster: Interview Center
interview.monster.com

Quintessential Careers: Job Interviewing Resources
www.quintcareers.com/intvres.html

Informational Interviews

Information Interviews (Florida State University)
www.career.fsu.edu/ccis/guides/infoint.html

Quintessential Careers: Informational Interviewing Tutorial
www.quintcareers.com/informational_interviewing.html

Job and Industry Information

American Society of Association Executives (ASAE)
www.asaenet.org

Career Guide to Industries
stats.bls.gov/oco/cg/home.htm

CareerOINK (information on 14,000 jobs)
www.careeroink.com

Hoover's Online (information on companies)
www.hoovers.com/free/

JIST Publishing (job search help; links to other sites)
www.jist.com

Occupational Information Network (O*NET)
online.onetcenter.org/

Occupational Outlook Handbook
www.bls.gov/oco

Company Information

CorporateInformation.com
www.corporateinformation.com

Dogpile (for finding specific company sites)
www.dogpile.com/

Google News
news.google.com

Industry Research Desk
www.virtualpet.com/industry/

Researching Companies Online
www.learnwebskills.com/company/

Riley Guide: Do the Research That Supports Your Job Search
www.rileyguide.com/jsresearch.html

SuperPages
www.superpages.com/

Thomas Register
www.thomasregister.com

Yahoo! News
news.yahoo.com/

Researching and Negotiating Salaries

Abbott, Langer & Associates
www.abbott-langer.com

America's Career InfoNet
www.acinet.org/acinet/

CareerOINK (includes average pay for all major jobs)
www.careeroink.com

JobStar Salary Information
jobstar.org/tools/salary/

Quintessential Careers' salary-negotiation tutorial
www.quintcareers.com/salary_negotiation.html

The Salary Calculator
www.homefair.com/calc/salcalc.html

Salary Expert
www.salaryexpert.com

Wageweb
www.wageweb.com

Finding and Applying for Job Openings

America's Job Bank (AJB)
www.ajb.dni.us

BestJobsUSA.com
www.bestjobsusa.com

CareerBuilder.com
www.careerbuilder.com

Careerbuzz
www.careerbuzz.com

CareerShop
www.careershop.com

CareerSite
www.careersite.com

FlipDog.com
flipdog.monster.com/

JobBank USA
www.jobbankusa.com

Monster
www.monster.com

NationJob
www.nationjob.com

Vault
www.vault.com

Yahoo! HotJobs
hotjobs.yahoo.com/

Index

X–Z

JIST Order and Catalog Request Form

Key Code: LP

Purchase Order #: _____
(Required by some organizations)

Billing Information

Organization Name: _____
Accounting Contact: _____
Street Address: _____
_____
_____
City, State, ZIP: _____
Phone Number: ( ) _____

Please copy this form if you need more lines for your order.

Phone: 1-800-648-JIST
Fax: 1-800-JIST-FAX
World Wide Web Address:
www.jist.com

Shipping Information with Street Address
(If Different from Above)

Organization Name: _____
Contact: _____
Street Address: (We *cannot* ship to P.O. boxes) _____
_____
_____
City, State, ZIP: _____
Phone Number: ( ) _____

Credit Card Purchases:
VISA _____ MC _____ AMEX _____
Card Number: _____
Exp. Date: _____
Name As on Card: _____
Signature: _____

Quantity	Order Code	Product Title	Unit Price	Total

jist Publishing
8902 Otis Avenue
Indianapolis, IN 46216

Shipping Fees

In the continental U.S. add 7% of subtotal:
- Minimum amount charged = $5.00
- FREE shipping and handling on any prepaid orders over $50.00

Above pricing is for regular ground shipment only. For rush or special delivery, call JIST Customer Service at 1-800-648-JIST for the correct shipping fee.

Outside the continental U.S. call JIST Customer Service at 1-800-648-JIST for an estimate of these fees.

Payment in U.S. funds only!

Subtotal	
+Shipping (See left)	
+6% Sales Tax *Indiana Residents*	
TOTAL	

JIST thanks you for your order!